DATE DUE

OCT 1 6 1985		
NOV 5 1986		
JUL 2 1987		
FEB 2 6 1988		
MAR 2 1 1988		
JUN 3 - 1988		
MAR 3 0 1989		
JUN 1 0 1994		
NOV 2 3 1994		
JAN - 8 1996		

DEMCO 38-297

ART PLASTIC

DESIGNED FOR LIVING

By Andrea DiNoto

Principal photography by David Arky

ART PLASTIC

DESIGNED FOR LIVING

Abbeville Press • Publishers • New York

Editor: Walton Rawls
Designer: Howard Morris
Assistant Designer: Victoria Arthur

Frontispiece: the Panton chair, photo courtesy of Herman Miller, Inc.

All photographs by David Arky unless otherwise noted in the captions.

Reprints from *Durez Plastics News* on pages 95, 97, 123, 126, 138, 139, 145, and 150 are used courtesy of Durez Resins & Molding Materials Division, Occidental Chemical Corporation.

Quotations on pages 178–179 from *Madame* by Patrick O'Higgins, © 1971 by Patrick O'Higgins, is reprinted by permission of Viking Penguin, Inc.

Library of Congress Cataloging in Publication Data

DiNoto, Andrea.
  Art plastic.

  Bibliography: p.
  Includes index.
  1. Plastics.   2. House furnishings.   I. Title.
TP1122.D56   1984   745.2   83-73418
ISBN 0-89659-437-8

Contents

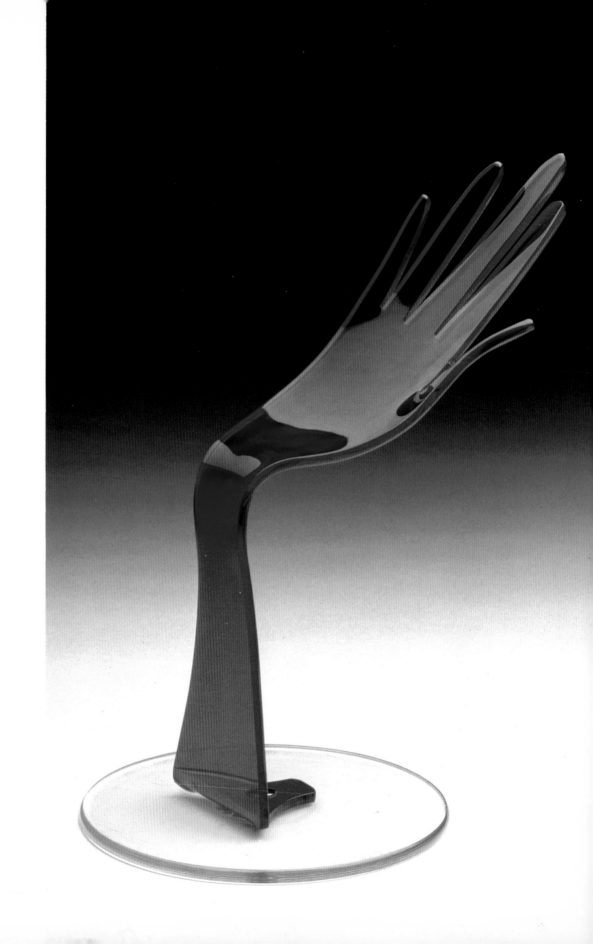

PREFACE

When I asked the saleswoman in a Madison Avenue boutique if I might see the plastic bracelets in the window, she retrieved them for me with the explanation, "They are not plastic, dear. They are Lucite." That was in the summer of 1982, when I had just begun the research for this book. Caught up in my subject I cheerfully countered, "But Lucite *is* plastic!" The woman's lips formed a frosty "Oh?," and as she plucked the bangles from my hands it became glaringly clear that I had committed a double gaffe: first by presuming to correct a common misconception about plastics; and secondly by just breathing that word—with its connotations of cheap and shoddy—in such elegant surroundings.

However, there was a time in the early decades of this century when plastics were viewed more felicitously. In 1936, no less an arbiter than *Fortune* magazine called the new materials "glamorous substances," precisely because they were man-made. But immediately after the second World War, manufacturers flooded the market with flimsy plastic goods that effectively came to symbolize—and trivialize—plastics in the minds of consumers. Compounding this problem, of course, was the seemingly indestructible nature of some plastics and their looming presence as the most all-pervasive, possibly permanent form of litter in the environment.

Not surprisingly, negative attitudes toward plastics continue to range from outright hostility to simple indifference, despite the growing importance of plastic materials in our lives. Plastic prejudice is particularly strong in the decorative arts, where for centuries natural materials and handcraftsmanship have held sway. And yet, since about the mid-nineteen-twenties, plastics have played increasingly important roles in the design of modern furniture and accessories, personal accoutrements, and, of course, utilitarian consumer goods. The moldability of plastics—together with such practical features as their strength and their moisture and chemical resistance—has enabled designers to transform

1. This acrylic display piece was made in Italy, probably in the 1940s, when the disembodied, stylized hand was a favorite surrealistic image. *Fred Silberman*

2

the most banal items into sculptural mass-produced "art" objects that we now view as icons of machine-age culture. The adaptability of plastics has, at the same time, led them to be accepted as a fine arts medium by both sculptors and painters; but the "art" implied by the title of this book refers almost exclusively to the art of the machine, of the designer, of the mold-maker; and of the unvarying multiples that result from this partnership.

How does one become interested in plastics? A sense of humor, an awareness of design, and ample curiosity about materials may be regarded as prerequisites. My own interest stemmed from my collection of Depression-era plastic jewelry gleaned from flea markets and street fairs. The bracelets and pins had a chunky, colorful style that made them very appealing; yet no one seemed to know all that much about the material. Dealers told me that pieces were hand-carved and that the substance was variously "Bakelite" or "Celluloid." But when questioned further, no one really knew for sure what the "stuff" was.

When I turned to books on plastics I found that most were written for and by industry professionals—chemists and engineers—in highly technical language and illustrated with formulas and pictures of processing machinery and industrial products. Plastic, I learned, was not one but a family of materials. The very few books devoted exclusively to plastics as a design medium also emphasized technology, although illustrations were at least geared to consumer products, albeit with an emphasis on the era following World

3

War II (see titles by Sylvia Katz and Thelma Newman in Bibliography). Only one book, *Plastics History USA* by J. Harry DuBois, gave an overview of the development of the plastics industry in America, and it also emphasized technological rather than design history. But, as I came to realize, the relationship between the two is inextricable; and it is only by understanding the technology and its implications in merchandising that decorative, or

formal, considerations begin to make sense. Eventually meeting Mr. DuBois, I learned that he (a retired engineer known in the industry as "Mr. Plastic") was instrumental in assembling the first exclusively plastic collection for the Smithsonian Institution in Washington, D.C. In permitting me to photograph plastic antiques from his own collection, he provided this book with its historical foundation.

While research had plunged me into

2. Charles Eames's shell chair, with seat and back molded of one piece of fiberglass-reinforced polyester resin, was the first plastic furniture design to be successfully mass-produced. Manufactured by the Herman Miller Company of Zeeland, Michigan, since 1949, it came in many variations. *Photo: Herman Miller Company*

3. Helix, a clock created by California designer Steve Diskin, utilizes three independently rotating spirals to tell hours, minutes, and seconds when read against the linear time scale. Thus, time progresses in a straight line as the spirals rotate, their movements mirrored in the polished chrome base. Spiral segments are made of injection-molded ABS plastic, and the whole is encased in a 23-inch acrylic tube. *Photo: Steve Diskin*

4

the literature of plastics, it also led me to discover a body of collectors whose interests seemed to focus on objects produced between the two world wars—what has come to be called the Machine Age. While many of these collectors shared my interest in jewelry, others concentrated on industrial design—utilitarian objects such as kitchen utensils and radios. I was fortunate early on to meet a European-born dealer in New York, Georg Kargl, who showed me a lavish catalog entitled *Bakeliet: Techniek/Vormgeving/Gebruik (Bakelite: Technique, Form, and Material)* produced by the prestigious Boymans-van Beuningen Museum in Rotterdam in 1981. Pictured was a collection of dark molded objects, many American-made, that included ordinary things like ashtrays, radios, and other electrical appliances manufactured roughly between 1930 and 1950. Many of the over-600 items in the exhibition had come from the collection of the well-known Dutch art collectors Agnes and Frits Becht, who had become fascinated with the sculptural quality of machine-made molded products. In presenting the collection, the museum saw an opportunity to highlight one area of industrial design and "show how complex and varied the objects produced in a simple material can be." (Bakelite was the first synthetic industrial plastic.) When another dealer, Gerard Widdershoven, brought me a catalog from a similar show at the Galerie Loft in Paris in 1982, I realized that Bakelite was indeed a collecting rage in Europe. It also became apparent that American collectors tended to value color while Europeans were more attracted to form. For example, in the U.S., collectors place a high value on colorful plastic radios produced during the 1930s and '40s; Europeans are more entranced by sleek, dark streamlined shapes. Both approaches are represented in *Art Plastic*, not only as a reflection of collecting trends but to give a more coherent view of plastics design history.

Although my original intent was to focus only on Machine Age design, I realized that collector interest in artifacts from the postwar decades was growing rapidly. This was dramatized when Manhattan's Greenwich Auction Room presented its "Fabulous Fifties" sale in 1983 (the first ever of "Fifties" objects) to a SRO crowd. Included in the sale were the furniture designs of Charles Eames and Eero Saarinen, whose plastic shell chairs caused a revolution in the furniture industry. Their concept of sculpturally molded mass-produced furniture led to the sensuous, flamboyant designs of the 1960s and

4. A washing-machine agitator molded by the Durez Plastics Division of Hooker Chemical is a good example of the accidental beauty of machine art. *Photo: Ferdinand Boesch, from the exhibition "Plastic as Plastic" at the American Craft Museum of the American Craft Council, 1968–69*

5. A polyethylene pitcher made by Minerware, Inc., is a Pop Art treasure found in a thrift shop. *Joan Baren*

'70s, many by Italians whose craft in plastics has become legendary. Works in rigid plastic or resilient foam were often inspired by Pop Art and Surrealism—see the "Marilyn" sofa on page 192—and while some of these designs have been in continual production since their introduction to the market, many are no longer available except in secondary markets. The Panton chair, for example, on page 182, was last produced in the U.S. in 1975 but has begun to appear in dealer's shops. At the same time, curators of twentieth-century decorative arts and design have begun to select these objects for shows such as the noteworthy "Design Since 1945" that opened at the Philadelphia Museum of Art in October, 1983. It seemed not only logical but essential to include a sampling of postwar plastics in this book as more and more they are drawn into the collecting spectrum.

Finally, I found it impossible to resist including at least a few examples of contemporary plastic design. Even though the range is much too vast to cover comprehensively in a book such as this, I felt it was important to suggest the scope of the immensely rich collecting area available to those with an eye for future rarities. Therefore, I have included such delights as the ubiquitous Gladys Goose (page 191), a good example of industrial folk art (not so different, really, from a 19th-century factory-made weathervane of copper hammered over a mold), and Steve Diskin's Helix clock, a design whose visual beauty and exquisitely subtle engineering is expressed through plastic materials.

As a result, this book became not only a collector's guide but something of a design history. It is admittedly idiosyncratic, reflecting my own taste and choices and those of the many other collectors whose objects are represented. No doubt some readers will be offended to see inexpensive novelties included between the same covers as "good design." But in my view the diversity and the mix are what make plastics design history interesting and the objects fun to contemplate and collect.

Inevitably this leads to the question of taste. For some people, anything purportedly "decorative" and made of plastic is automatic kitsch. However, one man's kitsch is another's cloisonné. Attitudes and opinions on art and design change constantly, and the question of what is or is not art or good taste becomes more and more subjective and somewhat academic. Even the word *kitsch* no longer connotes "bad taste" but is used more broadly by designers to indicate "popular culture." A plastic lawn flamingo taken out of its intended context could in fact be viewed as an art object. The fact that there is no flamingo in this book does not necessarily represent a critical judgment.

One can safely say, however, that there is no comparison to be made between plastics and natural materials. Plastics do not "breathe," they do not acquire a patina with age, they do not enjoy the mystique of ancientness that we confer on the noble naturals—glass, wood, ceramics, and metals. This, despite the fact that plastics are synthesized from the earth's most elemental substances: organic chemicals. Such is the contradictory and intriguing nature of plastics that inspired the French social theorist Roland Barthes to write in *Mythologies*, "Plastic . . . is the first magical substance that consents to be prosaic."

I hope, of course, that this book will present visual surprises and delights to those who had never considered the subject before. But I also intend for it to provide collectors with an introduction to the strange new vocabulary of synthetic materials that have so significantly infiltrated our lives even though their names and origins stubbornly remain a mystery. It was personally fascinating finally to discover what those household words "Celluloid" and "Bakelite" really signified, and to learn of their place in the establishment of a major industry. But it was ultimately most gratifying and interesting to examine the role of plastics as a medium in the decorative and industrial arts. Initially, what was most surprising to me, and to many of the people with whom I discussed this book, was the realization that the history of plastics dates back over 100 years, that there are indeed plastic *antiques* in the strict definition of the term. And while the thought may provoke a smile, one can indeed view the Machine Age alternatively as the Golden Age of Plastics. It was an era—filled as it was with streamlined fountain pens and chubby radios—when designers and consumers alike were discovering the awesome potential of man-made resins and the new esthetic of molded products.

6. Although this object might be viewed as an abstract Pop Art Mickey Mouse sculpture, it actually is a side table. Designed by Michele De Lucchi, member of the Milan-based international design group Memphis, it has a wood base covered in patterned plastic laminate and cartoonish legs of painted metal. *Photo: Memphis*

INTRODUCTION

When the Philadelphia Novelties Exhibition opened at the Franklin Institute in November, 1885, a reporter from *Frank Leslie's Illustrated Newspaper* wrote glowingly of "a wonderful material" presented in an elaborate display by the American Celluloid Company: ". . . their exhibition was a great revelation to those who are not familiar with the great variety of uses that celluloid is put to. It enters into an infinite number of articles for use in ornament, among which are brushes, combs, hand mirrors, jewelry, corkscrews, card and soap cases, powder boxes, pen racks, paper knives, thimbles, chess men, checkers, shoe hooks and horns, napkin rings, glove stretchers, parasol, umbrella, and cane handles, mouthpieces for pipes, collars and cuffs, knife handles for table cutlery, keys for pianos, organs, musical instruments and organ stops, martingale rings and harness trimmings, white and colored letters for signs, stereotype plates to print from, billiard pool balls, trusses and surgical instruments, frames for eyeglasses, plates for false teeth, emery wheels, whip handles, carriage mounting, corset clasps . . . etc. The above goods are not made in white alone but are in imitation of ivory, horn, agate, carnelian, amber, coral, precious marbles, etc., as well as in plain shades of colors, the company showing among its exhibits samples of over two-hundred colors among those which are regularly made." The reporter went on to describe the elegant exhibition space, outfitted with Brussels carpets and mahogany cases in which all these marvels were displayed. "The whole was enclosed with mahogany posts," he concluded, "surmounted with large balls of celluloid in imitation of ivory, tortoiseshell, malachite, etc., and paneled with celluloid marble, while between the posts hung a heavy cable chain of ivory celluloid, the whole containing one of the very handsomest exhibits which has ever been placed on view at a public exhibition. . . ."

The First Man-made Plastic

Celluloid was the American trade name for the first commercially successful

7. A child's rattle in the shape of the puppet Punch is formed of hand-painted Celluloid and dates from about 1910. Nine inches high, it is rare both for its size and mint condition. It is probably English. *Photo: Bartholomew Fair, Ltd.*

8

9

8–10. Molded shellac items from the 19th century include a picture frame dated Dec. 15, 1869, a tape measure, and a 4 x 5 inch daguerreotype case marked "F. B. Smith & Hartmann N. Y." The crisp detailing of each design demonstrates the excellent molding properties of shellac. *J. Harry duBois*

10

man-made material. It was the marvel, and the novelty, of the age; an entirely new material that could be formed into almost any shape, as the Franklin Institute exhibition showed. It was also only the first of dozens of new synthetics, called plastics, to emerge before the first-half of the 20th century. By the end of World War II many more had been developed, and today there are literally thousands of plastics beyond the few that most of us can name, albeit without any real understanding of their nature or why they exist at all.

The impetus to develop the first plastics came from the need to find a substitute for dwindling supplies of natural materials such as ivory and tortoiseshell, which always had been in great demand for luxury objects such as decorative combs and cutlery handles. In the 1840s, the Swiss chemist Christian Schoenbine had developed cellulose nitrate, obtained when wood or cotton fibers were acted upon by nitric and sulphuric acids. (Legend has it that he happened upon the discovery accidentally while mopping up spilled acid with his wife's apron.) The result was a highly flammable doughy substance that came to be used primarily for explosives. However, its moldable properties began to interest some inventors, who sought additional uses for it. In 1855, an Englishman, Alexander Parkes, succeeded in developing a form of cellulose nitrate that he called Parkesine, from which he made a number of beautifully colored, molded objects such as buttons, pens, medallions, and combs. Parkes's formula utilized small amounts of camphor as a solvent, a necessary additive that acted

as a thinner to bring the raw material to flowable consistency. Ultimately, Parkes failed to make a commercial success of Parkesine and permitted another Englishman, Daniel Spill, to produce it in his own factory under the names Xylonite and Ivoride. But over a period of several years, from 1865 to 1891, Spill's business suffered major setbacks associated with financing and patent infringement wars from which he never recovered.

About the time that Spill had begun the manufacture of Parkesine in England, an American inventor, John Wesley Hyatt, became interested in creating a substitute for ivory, when, in 1863, a billiard ball firm offered a prize of $10,000 for such a substance. Hyatt accepted the challenge, and though he did not win the prize (the actual winner is unknown) his experiments yielded a ball with a core of molded gum shellac and pulp. It was coated with collodion, a solution of cellulose nitrate and alcohol that dries on contact with air to a thin film. It was, like cellulose nitrate, highly flammable, and, unfortunately, when balls hit against each other during play the collodion often would explode with a mild detonation that sounded like a gunshot. In an oft-quoted anecdote, Hyatt reported: ". . . we had a letter from a billiard saloon proprietor in Colorado mentioning this fact . . . and saying he did not care so much about it, but that instantly every man in the room pulled a gun."

This and other problems of cellulose nitrate caused Hyatt and his brother Isaiah to experiment further. In *Plastics History USA*, J. Harry DuBois opines that while Hyatt may never actually have

seen the English papers of Parkes and Spill, he was probably, "as a prudent business man . . . not ignorant of the efforts of others in the field." In 1870, Hyatt obtained a patent for "Celluloid"— a trade name coined by his brother— a substance essentially the same as Parkesine and Xylonite, all of which utilized the same amount of camphor as a solvent. But Hyatt's improved formula was crucial in his winning a long and bitter patent infringement case brought against him by Spill. Although Spill had first established British patents in 1867 and 1869 and American patents in 1869 and 1870, and had initially won his suit in 1880, he ultimately lost when the same judge reversed his decision in favor of Hyatt in 1884.

Hyatt is therefore credited as the inventor of "Celluloid." This material provided the basis for the empire he established with his brother in 1871 upon forming the American Celluloid Company, today the Plastics Division of the Celanese Corporation.

Much of Hyatt's success is attributable to his early realization of the importance of developing advanced molding technology for the new materials, and to that end he worked closely with Charles Burroughs, an engineer and founder of the Burroughs Company, manufacturers of office machines. Together, they developed the first extrusion and compression molding machines, which were the forerunners of modern injection-molding methods (see *Glossary*). Hyatt also devised the blow-molding process in which a hollow tube of Celluloid, held in a special press, was heated and then inflated with hot air until the tube conformed to

The Nature of Plastics

A plastic (from the Greek *plastikos*, to mold or form) is broadly defined as any inherently formless material that can be molded or modeled. This might include clay, metals like lead, wax, or cement; but a more limited categorization connotes a certain group of substances that can be formed under heat and pressure. This includes natural plastics such as the group of fossilized tree resins commonly called amber; animal protein such as horn and tortoiseshell; and shellac, an insect secretion that, when mixed with a filler such as wood flour, acquires excellent molding properties. Gutta percha, a now obsolete substance obtained from Malayan trees, has the appearance of rubber and is sometimes included with the natural plastics. Rubber has plastic qualities, but because of its elasticity belongs to a related category, that of elastomers.

All plastics, whether natural or man-made are classified both according to how they respond to heat and by their special type of molecular structure. Plastics that repeatedly can be softened by heat, and thus re-formed, are called *thermoplastics*. They retain their plastic, or moldable, quality more or less indefinitely. Natural plastics and cellulosics are among the thermoplastics. In contrast, plastics that, once molded, can never be re-softened and returned to the moldable state are called *thermosets*. They can be charred or decomposed by high heat but never will become viscous again. They are, in effect, set for life. Bakelite, a phenolic resin, was the first synthetic thermosetting plastic.

All plastics, whether natural or synthetic, thermoplastic or thermoset, are defined as *polymers*, a term that describes a type of molecular structure. Polymers (from the Greek *poly*, many; *mer*, part) are giant molecules—actually only about 1/10,000th of an inch long—made up of many small molecules. A polymer forms when the carbon atoms of two or more organic (carbon-containing) substances combine to form an entirely new macro-molecule. The structure of a polymer can be imagined as a chain of paper clips. Millions of polymer chains can comprise a single object.

When polymer chains mass together, they can do so in a simple linear way, layer upon layer; or in a complex three-dimensional way, like a bowl of tangled spaghetti strands. En masse, either stacked up or tangled, the carbon atoms in the polymers tend naturally to combine further so that the chains are held together either (1) by a weak electromagnetic attraction, as is the case with simple thermoplastics like celluloid, or (2) by a strong, permanent, chemical bonding called cross-linking. Cross-link bonding ("spaghetti bowl") characterizes the complex thermosetting plastics like Bakelite. This explains why a thermoset cannot be melted down once formed. Heat will not destroy the cross-link bonding once it has been established. In thermoplastics, however, heat easily loosens the simple electromagnetic attractions between the carbon atoms and causes melting, which is actually evidence of the polymer chains separating.

Polymerization is today a highly sophisticated science that enables chemists to, in effect, "breed" plastics with specific properties by creating what has been called the "tailor-made molecule." But until the 1920s polymeric principles were little understood, and early experiments in plastics were done most often by amateur inventors who saw commercial possibilities in expanding the roles of natural and synthetic resins.

11

11. The inventor of Celluloid, John Wesley Hyatt (1837–1920), is also credited with the development of many basic plastics processing methods. *Photo: Celanese Plastics Division*

12. Celluloid baby rattles depicting children playing musical instruments date from about 1890 and were among the first plastic products to be made by the blow-molding technique. *Photo: Celanese Plastics Division*

12

the shape of the surrounding mold. The result was a three-dimensional hollow object of great delicacy. The principle is still used today.

In manufacture, Celluloid usually was first formed into blocks from which thin sheets were planed. These sheets could be stamped to form trays, picture frames, and the like, or used to cover wooden handles in imitation of ivory. The French are credited with eventually improving upon this method by using thicker slabs of Celluloid for their "French Ivory" wares, typically vanity sets and jewelry, characterized by creamy coloring and delicate striations that are still mistaken for the natural veining of true ivory.

In 1896, a compendium entitled *The House and Home: A Practical Guide*, advised economy-minded women that "in cutlery handles, Celluloid is preferable to ivory; it does not crack or discolor and is not affected by hot water. So beautiful is the finish that only a connoisseur can tell it from real ivory. Knives and forks of medium quality of steel and best Celluloid handles sell at eight dollars and a half a dozen, while the same quality of steel in ivory costs twenty-eight dollars a dozen. No millionaire could buy a better carving set than may be had in this ware for five dollars and a half and they are in all respects preferable to solid silver."

Celluloid obviously had more than fulfilled its promise as a substitute and quickly became a worldwide phenomenon, with manufacturing plants established in England, Europe, and Japan. In America, Hyatt's competitors proliferated, including the Fiberloid Company (eventually Monsanto), which produced Celluloid collars and cuffs, the Foster Grant Company, Eastman Kodak, and many others. In 1910, the formidable munitions company E. I. Du Pont de Nemours entered the field with the purchase of the Arlington Company, makers of Pyroxylin (another trade name for cellulose nitrate). Du Pont also produced an imitation leather called Fabrikoid. The company's long involvement with nitrates, a basic ingredient of gunpowder and explosives, led them naturally to plastics research. Since 1906, Du Pont had been producing cellulose-based lacquers for metals, and by the early twenties their production of cellulosic plastic was to exceed that of all France. In an authorized history of the company, a footnote reveals that Du Pont was even making Celluloid bibs for nuns until well into the 1930s.

During the "Celluloid Era," dating roughly from the last decades of the 19th century through the early 1920s, production of the raw material peaked at 40,000 tons per year. The British plastics historian M. Kaufman reported in his book, *The First Century of Plastics*, that around the turn of the century women "carried a couple of pounds of Celluloid about their persons in the shape of many combs."

But while Celluloid was a versatile and beautiful material, it had one major drawback, particularly in film form: violent flammability. Because cellulosic film was colorless and transparent, it was used as window sheeting for buggies and automobiles, but more significantly as the first photographic film. It revolutionized the photography industry and gave birth to the movies. Be-

cause Celluloid film was always in close proximity to hot lights, devastating fires were alarmingly frequent until a way was found to substitute acetic acid (vinegar) for the volatile nitric acid in the Celluloid formula. In 1900, the French scientist Henri Dreyfuss perfected a process for producing the result, cellulose acetate, in film form. Called "safety film" even though it was not absolutely fireproof, the new material was immediately adopted by the film industry and its use enforced by law. Cellulose acetate had other advantages, including its ability to be spun into fibers from which the first rayon fabric was made. In dope form it also provided a hard nonflammable coating for airplane and automobile bodies. In the late 1920s, a method was developed by which it could be injection-molded, a mechanical process that quickly produces many identical objects simultaneously.

Protein Plastics

Chemical research into other types of synthetic resins was sometimes prompted by unaccountable motives. In 1897, two German scientists searching for a way in which to make white blackboards obtained a hornlike substance by combining casein, a milk protein, and formaldehyde. They patented it under the name Galalith (from the greek words *gala*, milk; and *litho*, stone), but in England it was called Erinoid, supposedly because the milk used came from Ireland. According to British plastics historian Sylvia Katz, Erinoid was first used in Great Britain in 1913 as a material for buttons, buckles, and jewelry and to produce millions of knitting needles and crochet

hooks during World War I "for women of England to knit woolies for the forces."

Casein was first manufactured in America in 1919 by, among others, the Aladdinite Company. The name was chosen, according to the manufacturer, because casein, "like Aladdin's lamp, needed to be polished to bring out its true value and beauty." Casein was used extensively by button manufacturers until the 1930s, but its primary employment today is as a base for paints and glues.

Other protein plastics that derived from soybeans and cereal products were tried briefly during World War II but with little success. They represented an interesting experiment, but one that ultimately had little lasting impact on the industry when compared with Celluloid and Bakelite.

The Bakelite Era

In 1907, Dr. Leo Baekeland invented the first entirely synthetic plastic. (Because Celluloid and protein plastics are based on plant and animal substances, they usually are classified as semi-synthetics.) It was a thermosetting resin that he patented in 1909 under the name Bakelite. It was the material that, in a much more significant way than Celluloid, inaugurated the modern plastics industry. Baekeland was a Belgian-born chemist of genius. Before concentrating on resins, he had invented and produced Velox photographic printing paper, which, in 1899, he sold to the Eastman Kodak Company for three-quarters of a million dollars. This considerable fortune left him free to pursue independent research for the rest of his life. Work-

13

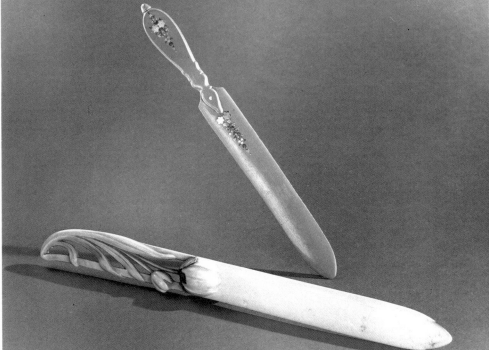

14

13. The figures carved into the handles of these c. 1920s vanity items suggest that they were made in Japan.

14. The Celluloid letter opener, top, is inlaid with copper and dates to 1874, when it was submitted with a patent application for metal inlays in plastics. The carved opener, below, dates to c. 1920. *Photos: Celanese Plastics Division*

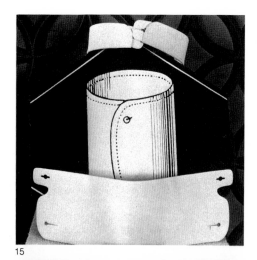

15

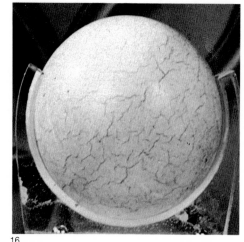

16

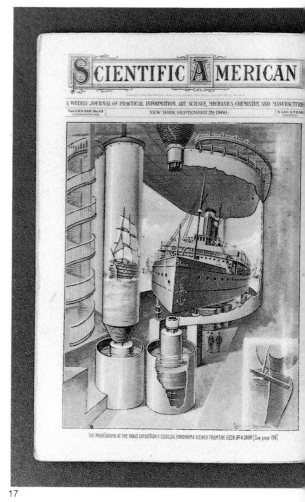

17

15. Celluloid collars and cuffs were a torturous fashion accessory that assured a wrinkle-free look.

16. John Wesley Hyatt, inventor of Celluloid, submitted this billiard ball made of solid cellulose nitrate with his patent application for that material in 1868.
Photos: Celanese Plastics Division

17. In 1900, *Scientific American* magazine offered this miniature Celluloid replica as a premium to new subscribers. Measuring only 2 x 3 inches, it is engraved with an actual cover illustration on the back. Subscription particulars are explained on the front and on the tissue pages stapled inside. *J. Harry DuBois*

ing in a small laboratory adjacent to his home in a fashionable section of Yonkers, New York, Baekeland took up a problem that for years had challenged and defeated other gifted researchers: the creation of a thermosetting resin from the reaction of phenol (carbolic acid) with formaldehyde. As J. H. DuBois recounts in *Plastics History USA*, Baekeland was interested initially in developing a shellac and varnish substitute. However, he quickly realized

that a resin that was both insoluble and infusible could have a much wider commercial application as a molding compound, especially for electrical insulation. Baekeland discovered for phenol and formaldehyde a suitable catalyst—a substance that speeds the union of ingredients but does not combine with them—and was the first to realize that only under extremely high heat and pressure would the resin polymerize as a thermoset.

The process by which phenolic resin is created was described in the May, 1940, issue of *Durez Plastics News*, the organ of one of Bakelite's major competitors. The two basic ingredients and a few other chemicals in small amounts are combined with a catalyst and cooked in a huge kettle until the substance becomes resinous. When dumped from the kettle, hot, this material has the consistency of cold molasses, and as it spreads over a flat surface it begins to harden almost immediately. It is very brittle, usually of a pale amber color, and resembles rosin or natural gums (which probably explains why the name resin was given to the material). To provide the resin with desirable molding qualities and color, it is necessary to add pigment and what is termed a filler. This filler may be wood flour, cotton flock, asbestos, mica, or a number of other things (including ground walnut shell). The one used most is wood flour—an exceedingly finely ground or powdered wood. The resin itself is ground to about the consistency of face powder before the coloring agent and filler are added, and the whole, after a thorough mixing, is passed through sifters and hoppers. But in that state it still would not cure or set in the mold fast enough, so it is necessary to advance the compound by putting it through hot mixing rolls from which it emerges in sheet form. At this point it has to be reground, which is done in huge grinding machines, and it is converted to a granular powder that is almost ready for the final blending. As it passes from these grinders it is carried over magnetic separators that remove bits of metal that might have been picked up during the processing and is delivered to the final blenders to assure a positive standard, a thoroughly dependable, uniform product. From the blenders it is placed in drums ready for shipment to the custom molder.

The first commercial application of Bakelite was, as Baekeland expected, as an alternative to rubber for electrical insulation. In 1910, the General Bakelite Corporation (which merged into Union Carbide in 1939) established

18

headquarters in Perth Amboy, New Jersey. There Baekeland produced the resin in various forms for many electrical companies (but also for the everenterprising billiard ball industry, which abandoned Celluloid in favor of Baekeland's much superior, more durable material). Baekeland was quick to set up branches of the company in Europe and built his first factory near Berlin. It was not until 1927, however, that he registered Bakelite, Ltd., in Great

18. This Art Nouveau picture frame, made in England of thermoformed Celluloid, has a hand-painted border. *J. Harry DuBois*

19

19. Celluloid postcards date from the Edwardian era. The folding fan—so elaborate it requires its own mailing box—was made by die-stamping thin sheets of Celluloid, which were then painted and threaded on satin ribbon and fastened to the card. The other, entirely hand-painted on a translucent sheet of Celluloid, is inscribed with a sentiment in French and dated 1909. *Author's collection*

Britain, where in the interim another gifted scientist, James Swinburne, had been conducting his own phenol–form-aldehyde researches. Swinburne had arrived at the same conclusions as Baekeland, but discovered, when he went to file his patent in 1907, that Baekeland's patent preceded his by one day. Nevertheless, from 1910 until his company was absorbed by Bakelite in 1927, Swinburne produced a valu-able phenolic lacquer called Damard

that was used for coating metals.

"The Material of a Thousand Uses"

Although Bakelite was always of pri-mary importance as an electrical insu-lation material, it was soon employed for everyday objects and dubbed by its promoters, "the material of a thou-sand uses." In many cases the objects made from it were not molded under high heat and pressure but cast. In the casting process, the viscous phenolic

20

21

syrup is simply poured into a lead mold and allowed to harden slowly. Castings have a markedly different appearance from moldings.

Cast phenolic resin (now rarely produced) had basically the same ingredients as the molding resin; but by slightly varying the base mixture and adding coloring agents it could be produced in every color, including clear and white, and in delicate pastels and vivid jewel-like hues. If no fillers were used it was transparent or translucent. But it also could be opaque. Mottling and other multicolored effects could be created by stirring a special liquid into the resin before it was poured into lead molds and cured in ovens until it had polymerized and hardened. Castings were often in the shape of rods and cylinders, letters of the alphabet (from which lettering for signs was made), but in many other shapes as well. In 1937, *Modern Plastics* magazine estimated that of the 5½ million pounds of cast resin produced that year, about 40 to 45 percent was used by the button industry and 7 to 9 percent for costume

jewelry. It was also used widely for handles, knobs, pulls, smoking equipment, desk sets, and game pieces such as poker chips and chessmen.

The resin was also used as an adhesive in the creation of laminates such as plywood and Formica. In the laminating process, sheets of a base material are impregnated with the resin, then multiple layers are bonded together under pressure to form a rigid, strong, moisture-resistant composite sheet about 1/16 of an inch thick.

The "Beetle" Revolution

Bakelite was the plastic industry's wunderkind, but as a molding material it had a limited color range. Even the dark colors that were possible were unstable and tended to fade on exposure to sunlight; pastels and a pure white could not be obtained at all. In 1924, a British scientist successfully substituted urea (ammonia and carbon dioxide) for phenol in the formaldehyde formula and obtained a thermosetting molding powder that made a new color range, including white, possible for the

20. Phenolic parasol handles date from about 1910 and demonstrate the early use of synthetic resin for decorative purposes.

21. A wall bracket, c. 1920, was the first application of a phenolic molded part for a household lighting fixture. *Photos: Union Carbide Corporation*

first time. Like phenol-formaldehyde, the urea resin had good heat resistance, rigidity, and surface hardness. It was first manufactured as "Beetle" by the British Cyanides Company. In *Plastics: Designs and Materials*, Sylvia Katz reports that it was displayed for the first time at the Wembley Exhibition in 1925 and hailed as "the new white hope."

The British manufacturers of Beetleware were so enthusiastic about the new material that in 1929 they opened a retail shop in London's bustling Regent Street devoted entirely to products made of molded synthetic resin. The December, 1929, issue of *Plastics* magazine reported that "the establishment is known as the 'Beatl' shop; the object of the shop is, of course, to sell Beatl moldings to the vast consuming public of London. . . . The first ads simply informed the public in large type that 'the Beatl Shop is Open,' the word 'Beatl' being calculated to arouse the curiosity of the public. This psychology proved correct, for those who did not know what

'Beatl' was turned up in vast numbers to repair their ignorance. . . ."

By 1929, the American Cyanamid Company had purchased patent rights to the "Beetle" formula and production began in the United States. As in England where it was marketed under several trade names—including "Beatl," "Beetleware," "Bandalasta," and "Linga Longa"—urea-formaldehyde products were at first largely limited to tableware such as cups, bowls, and tumblers. But in 1934 it was used historically for the first large-scale all-white housing for a countertop scale produced by the Toledo Scale Company. The molding required a solid steel press two stories high that exerted a pressure of 1,520 tons. Like phenolic resin (Bakelite), urea-formaldehyde required this enormous pressure to polymerize; and in the case of a large molding—actually only a few square feet—the size of the press had to be increased proportionately in order to supply the required pounds per square inch (psi). The scale

represented a milestone in molding technology and proved that, despite the great cost of the tooling, the product, at less than half the weight of the previous cast-iron model, would sell three times as fast. The lighter weight permitted salesmen to carry samples more easily and hence visit more prospective clients in a day.

Urea-formaldehyde moldings were also used widely on small electrical appliances such as shavers and hair dryers and thus began to bring the all-white hygienic look to personal items as well. As a material, urea was least successful in applications where it came into fairly constant contact with hot and cold liquid. The cellulosic fillers (such as wood flour or pulp) commonly used in the preparation of "Beetle" powders had poor moisture resistance and caused cups and other types of dinnerware to fade and crack.

Melamine: A Better Beetle

In 1937 a new thermosetting molding compound called melamine was introduced by American Cyanamid. It had been synthesized in 1834, but more than 100 years had elapsed before a way was found to produce it in mass quantities. Melamine, unlike phenolic and urea resins, could be prepared with mineral fillers, resulting in markedly increased moisture, acid, and heat resistance. Minerals also improved color stability and abrasion resistance, two factors that figured importantly in its use for tableware. But like phenolic resin it also found wide application in the preparation of decorative laminates.

Petrochemical Plastics

Between 1927 and the onset of World War II, a number of other important new plastics were developed whose essential ingredients derived from petrochemicals—essentially coal tar distillates. Among those most familiar to consumers are vinyl, acrylic, polystyrene, nylon, polyester, and polyethylene. All are in use today for both industrial and consumer products. Their special properties include extreme toughness combined with flexibility, the ability to

be produced in many forms (sheet, film, strand, etc.); and, in the case of acrylic, excellent optical clarity. Prewar use of these and previously invented plastics was largely experimental, and it took the wartime shortages of traditional materials to catalyze researches into improved fabrication techniques. Du Pont produced enough acrylic—under their trade name "Lucite" —during the war to make 370,000 bomber nose cones and gun turrets. In *Plastics History USA*, DuBois notes that cellulosics were used for "ammunition feed rollers, visors, scabbards, bullet-core tips, urinals, bugles, canteens, instrument and machine components and gas masks." Vinyl made safety glass possible—a thin film sandwiched between layers of glass prevented shattering. Melamine was an important insulation material and also was used in motors for molded distributor housings.

Among the new plastics developed during the war were silicones, epoxies, foamed plastics such as polyurethane, glass-reinforced plastics, and synthetic rubber. Between 1945 and the mid-1970s, the plastics industry grew at the phenomenal rate of 15 percent per year into a multibillion dollar industry with applications that touch every part of our lives. Many tailor-made plastics today can no longer be simply described by early criteria of thermoset or thermoplastic because they now can be made to combine seemingly contradictory properties. For example, co-extrusion makes it possible to build a plastic that simultaneously combines layers of specifically different materials, each of which provides a different property, e.g., one layer could be water

24

22. The Bakelite Corporation produced these promotional catalogs in an effort to educate the public about "The material of a thousand uses." Printed in color, the catalogs are rare examples of plastic ephemera. *J. Harry DuBois*

23. Dr. Leo H. Baekeland, inventor of Bakelite, is pictured with his wife and daughters, in the first decade of this century, in front of their Yonkers, N.Y., home. *J. Harry DuBois*

24. The original reactor used by Dr. Baekeland in 1908 to produce the first batch of phenolic resin, Bakelite, is owned by Union Carbide. The first semi-commercial equipment of its kind ever built, it turned out about 350 pounds of resin a day and was in use until well into the 1950s. *Photo: Union Carbide Corporation*

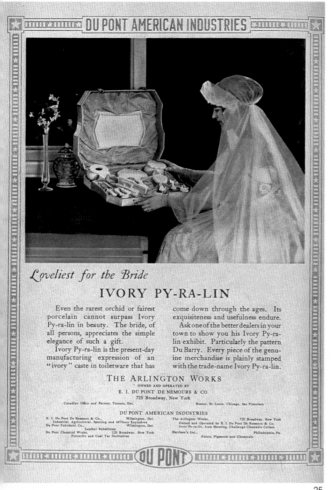

25

25. A Du Pont advertisement from 1918 promotes Py-ra-lin, the company's version of Celluloid. The ivorylike material is shown in the form of a vanity set suitable for the loveliest bride. *Photo: Eleutherian Mills/Hagley Foundation*

resistant, another bulletproof, another tinted to block ultraviolet light, another impact resistant, and so forth.

Styles of Plastics

Manufacturers of the earliest plastics were essentially businessmen with a desire to satisfy popular tastes. Therefore, they did their best to duplicate in plastic the prevailing Victorian and Edwardian styles of ornament that dominated the late-19th and early-20th centuries. They would be puzzled by the outcry of contemporary critics denouncing the use of plastics as imitative materials. Their good imitations of ivory, amber, tortoiseshell, and mother-of-pearl sold very well, particularly in the form of vanity sets to which they gave impressive-sounding, elegant names like Sheraton, DuBarry, and Wedgwood. Why not have cheap versions of the real thing if that is what people wanted, and if they could be manufactured with some degree of taste? This line of reasoning persisted as regards the modern style, now called Art Deco, that debuted at the Paris Exhibition of 1925. Plastic jewelry and novelty manufacturers in particular were entranced by the brilliant colors, simplified forms, and exotic motifs of the style. But even fine designers began to view synthetics such as Celluloid and Bakelite as appropriate materials for high-quality decorative wares.

The Art Deco mode, called Moderne in America, introduced stylized abstract and geometrical forms derived from Cubist art—which in turn had borrowed freely from primitive art. Stepped architectural forms and motifs were drawn from Mayan, Aztec, and Egyptian cultures. Stylized floral patterns were derived from Japanese prints and textiles and also from the late-19th-century Viennese Arts and Crafts Movement. Zigzags, lightning bolts, stylized fountains and sunbursts alluded to the electrifying atmosphere of the modern age and the popular cults of nature worship and sunbathing. The vivid color palette of Art Deco derived largely from the stage and costume designs of Leon Bakst for the Ballets Russes de Monte Carlo introduced to Parisians in 1909, but also from Oriental and Persian examples. The furniture and objects that embodied this diverse and exciting imagery purported to be expressive of the new Machine Age but were in fact reworkings of the Empire style and entirely handmade from rare and precious materials. This unabashed opulence not only smacked of old-world elitism but stood in flagrant contrast to Modernism, a philosophy of design that had been developing in Europe since the first decade of the 20th century. As early as 1909, the Futurists, a group of avant-garde Italian artists, had published a manifesto that made a strong impression on European art and architecture. They called for a rejection of past styles and mores and expressed an unbridled enthusiasm for speed and the *dinamismo* of the machine. In 1914, the Futurist architect Sant' Elia envisioned a house "like a giant machine, without painting or sculpture, enriched only by the innate beauty of its lines, extraordinarily brutal in its mechanical simplicity." A few years later the influential French architect Le Corbusier coined the phrase for all time: "A house is a machine for living in."

26

Underlying these stark pronouncements—which spawned the phrases "brutalism" and "purism"—was a sense of social responsibility and a belief in the democratizing effects of standardization, mass-production, and the use of industrial materials available to all. This machine esthetic was governed by principles of form, function, and space that were redefining the architecture of the 20th century. The Bauhaus, a small architectural and design school established in 1919 in Weimar, Germany, by Walter Gropius, gave coherence to these ideas under the banner of Functionalism. The Bauhaus set many ambitious goals, including the creation of prototype household objects suitable for mass production. Few were actually produced because the school, viewed as Communistic by the Nazis, was closed in 1933. At that time several of its most prominent teachers emigrated to the United States. Still, the few prototypes that were produced have become classics of modern design. The most famous example is perhaps the austere tubular steel furniture designed by Marcel Breuer around 1925 and produced by Thonet, the firm that had introduced bentwood furniture in the 19th century. (Today both Thonet and Knoll produce Breuer's designs.)

Many young designers were impressed with the Bauhaus philosophy, particularly the use of industrial materials such as steel for furniture design. Paul T. Frankl, one of the leading American émigrée designers of the period, wrote in 1930: "These new materials are expressive of our own age. They speak in the vernacular of the 20th century. Theirs is the language of invention, of synthesis. Industrial chemistry today rivals alchemy! Base materials are transmuted into marvels of new beauty." Frankl was referring to the use of new metals such as chrome and monel, and also to plastics in laminate form that were being used for the first time to surface tabletops and even entire walls by the early thirties. Some designers, however, achieved striking results by using plastics within an established decorative arts tradition such as bookbinding. In France, in particular, during the twenties bookbinders used rare, exotic, and unusual materials, including plastics, either as ornament or for the entire binding. (In the late forties and fifties, the binder Henri Merchere produced handpainted acrylic bindings that are unusual examples of the art.) In contrast to these luxury plastics was the mass-produced plastic spiral binding, an innovation of the twenties that, with its mechanical and purely functional design, was more in the spirit of the Bauhaus.

As designers like Frankl interpreted the new styles for clients not used to the severity of Functionalism, the rectilinear lines were inevitably softened. In working with tubular steel, for example, the Bauhaus right-angle was commonly transformed into a graceful "U" thought to be more "decorative." Also, elements of Art Deco, such as zebra skins, were sometimes introduced to add a touch of the exotic. The result of such a melding was called *modernistic*. From the Bauhaus point of view this was a derogatory term implying a phony kind of modernism. In 1938, John McAndrew, curator of architecture and industrial art

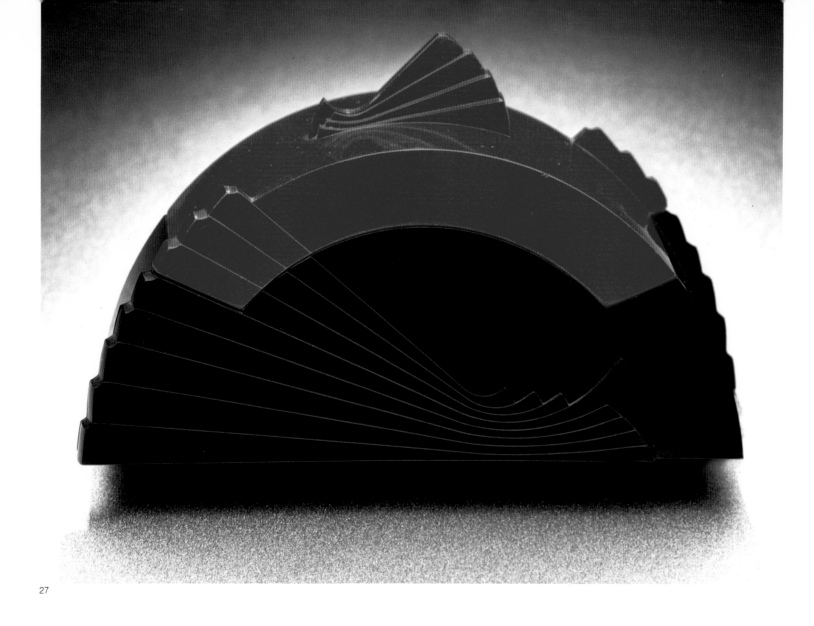

27. In 1935, the General Electric Co. Plastics Division molded this striking Art Deco box—advertised as the "Cleopatra Manicure Box"—of reinforced phenolic resin normally used for electrical insulation. *Primavera Gallery*

28. Oriental curios of hand-carved ivorylike Celluloid were popular in the 1920s and '30s when this figure was made. They are among the most convincing ivory imitations. *Dom La Raia*

at the Museum of Modern Art, wrote in the museum bulletin that "*modernistic* should apply to works which imitate superficially the forms of modern art, reducing them to decorative mannerism." Writing a decade later in *The Tastemakers*, Russell Lynes recalled that "'modernistic' was the bane of the existence of those who were seriously trying to promote 'modern'" and that the former was "typified by the bookcase that stepped up like a skyscraper and was capped with a copy of an African mask. . . . " (Skyscraper furniture was a specialty of Paul Frankl and is in great demand by collectors today.)

Consumers who had been viewing the varieties of modern furniture since the late twenties at department store exhibitions were undoubtedly confused by the terminology. In November, 1935, *Fortune* magazine tried to sort things out in an article entitled "What d'You Mean, Modern?" but only made matters worse by offering another made-up term, *modernisme*, which was unhelpfully defined as "a screwy, not necessarily unpleasant scramble of the 'modernized.'" As an example of true modern, however, *Fortune* presented several interior plans by the noted American designer Gilbert Rohde that featured clean, spare yet comfortable furnishings set in simple, workable floor plans. Absent was the glamor of mirrored walls, high-gloss lacquered furniture, zebra skins, and other exotic touches that tended to characterize the moderne. (In his book, *Depression Modern*, Martin Grief observes that during the thirties Hollywood set designers invariably used the moderne to create sexy boudoirs for voluptuous femme fatales like Mae West, leaving virtuous wives to languish amidst chintz curtains and Colonial furniture.)

The Streamlined Style

The ideas of Modernism had a great influence on the styling, or restyling, of everyday objects, which commenced with the onset of the Depression and the subsequent rise of the industrial design profession *and* the growth of the plastics industry. The founding fathers of industrial design in America—Raymond Loewy, Harold Van Doren, Norman Bel Geddes, and Walter Dorwin Teague—all had come from backgrounds in commercial art, advertising, or stage design, professions that demanded a combination of keen graphic sense and showmanship. They were lured to industry to help redesign and restyle products to give them "sales appeal" in the competitive and floundering Depression economy. Individually

they worked as consultants to many firms at once, applying their skills to diverse products, "everything," as Raymond Loewy put it, "from a lipstick to a locomotive." Most insisted on working closely with engineers so as to better relate design to function; but their primary task was to produce an eye-catching package.

Plastics, with their ease of mass production and color potential, fell conveniently into this scenario. So did the streamlined style, a phenomenon that arose out of scientific research into the perfect aerodynamic form. The *Oxford English Dictionary* defines streamlined as "that shape of solid body which is calculated to meet with the smallest amount of resistance in passing through the atmosphere." Since the late 19th century, scientists and engineers had been experimenting with the application of organic forms—of fish, for example—to moving vehicles in the interest of increased speed and efficiency. The streamline was an abstraction of these organic shapes, a graceful elliptical curve tapered at the end and resembling a teardrop. It was intended as a purely functional form, and applications often produced bizarre results such as blunt-nosed, steel-clad, three-wheeled vehicles resembling giant mechanical rolling fish. One of the most famous was Buckminster Fuller's Dymaxion car unveiled at the 1934 Chicago World's Fair. In 1938, the 20th Century Limited, the train that ran between New York and Chicago, became the first "streamliner" to be put into commercial operation. Streamlining quickly came to symbolize the aspirations of the new machine age: speed,

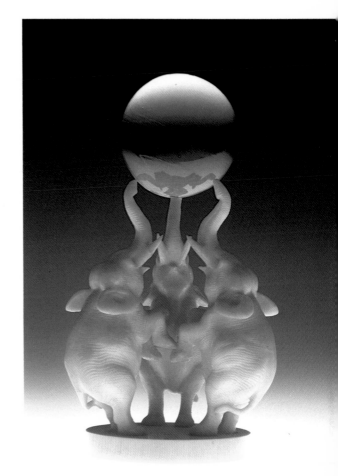

28

grace, and forward movement. It understandably fascinated science-fiction artists and writers, as did the notion of plastics with their colors and flowing properties. In 1942, the Englishman Frank R. Paul described *London of the Future* as ". . . a city of cast and rolled plastic materials of brilliant and beautiful colors. It is a city of curves and streamlines, of sweep and rounded beauty . . . a miracle of architecture . . . a mecca of peace, quiet, and content-

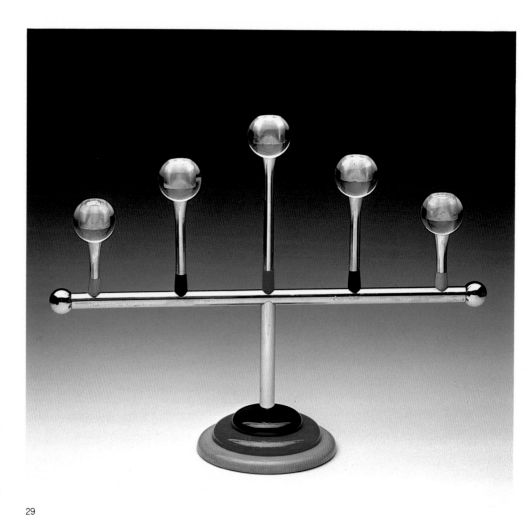

29. An unusual candelabrum from the 1930s or '40s combines chrome and plastic for a look of luxury. *Richard Utilla*

30–31. Two pairs of whimsical bookends by the American chromeware manufacturer Chase utilize plastic to dramatize the abstract metal forms. *Richard Utilla*

29

ment, and a wonderhouse of science and industry and mechanical coordination. It is Man's Utopia at last."

Industrial designers also saw a dynamic beauty in the line and began applying it decoratively to stationary objects. Appliances, fountain pens, and even toys were streamlined with dramatic results. In 1936, *Modern Plastics* magazine instituted an annual design awards competition that was won the following year by the E. H. Hotchkiss

Company for its streamlined stapler.

Walter Dorwin Teague called streamlining "characteristic of our age," and in his book *Design This Day* wrote that it "expresses force and grace in whatever form it defines. . . . there is surely no more exciting form in modern design."

To the strict Functionalist, it was just another mannerism, however. But when its popularity began to fade with the onset of World War II, the reasons were

more related to disillusionment—the failure of the machine to deliver a trouble-free Utopia—than with esthetic considerations. Also, as Jeffrey Meikle points out in *20th Century Limited*, the style became "discredited owing to its hints of totalitarianism in its smooth-flowing lines." Writing in *Mechanization Takes Command*, the architectural critic Sigfried Giedion conceded that the style "wielded a remarkable fascination" but felt its attempt to make objects appear

30

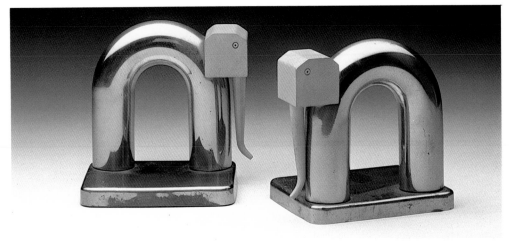

31

heavy and impressive overemphasized contours, resulting in a "bloated" look.

The style continues to fascinate collectors of plastics precisely because the material so well suited the style. The flowing streamline adapted perfectly to the requirements for plastic mold design in which sharp corners and edges were considered structurally weak. Domed or hemispherical shapes were stronger than flattened ones since they distributed weight and stress more

evenly. The ribbed pattern of three or more parallel lines running either vertically or horizontally was also a source of structural strength—not merely a design cliché as is sometimes stated. Also, soft edges and curves facilitated extraction from the mold and could easily be machine polished, which saved money. Even as streamlining began to fade in the late 1930s, the soft plastic curve persisted, although without such specific characteristics.

A more moderate approach, which in the mid-forties Henry Dreyfuss called "cleanlining," better described, in his view, what the industrial designers were trying to do with products that "haven't the faintest connection with speed through space." In retrospect, many industrial designers viewed streamlining of relatively stationary objects such as fountain pens and carpet sweepers as an embarrassment even though streamlining had given the decade one of the most compelling and unifying graphic symbols ever devised.

Postwar Design

New plastics and new technologies for forming and molding them again transformed the look of products—from housewares to office equipment to home furnishings—in the postwar decades. The industrial design profession expanded from a relatively small group of consultants into an international "college" of designers centered in the United States, Europe, Great Britain, Scandinavia, and Japan. Individual designers emerged as "stars" and innovators.

In the early 1950s, Charles Eames and Eero Saarinen produced the first chair with a shell made of fiberglass reinforced polyester (FRP), an innovation that revolutionized the mass production of furniture for homes and institutions. In the 1960s and '70s, a score of young Italian designers, including Marco Zanuso and Joe Columbo, dazzled the design world with an outpouring of flamboyant, sculptural, often humorous plastic furniture that poked

32

32. The elegant Sonora, made in France under an American license in 1945, is often called the "Cadillac" of radios. *Photo: Galerie Roudillon; Christian Gervais*

fun at the ascetic ideas of modernism. In Scandinavia, designers such as Carl-Arne Berger and Hugo Lindstrom were using plastics in the redesign of tools, house and institutional wares, and equipment for the handicapped. "Corporate identities" were created by designers such as Ettore Sottsass, Jr., for Olivetti, Eliot Noyes for IBM, and Dieter Rams for Braun—all of whom utilized the new light, strong, impact-resistant thermoplastics in the creation of elegant prod-

ucts with an instantly identifiable "look."

In 1951, an exhibition of plastic product design was presented by the Columbus Gallery of Fine Arts (now the Columbus Museum) in Ohio. Included were 175 everyday objects—including housewares, office equipment, furniture, jewelry, toys, textiles, and more—representing a survey of the new materials that the organizers hoped would stimulate further development of good design in the field. "It is undoubtedly too early

33. The Olivetti portable Valentine typewriter, designed by Ettore Sottsass, Jr., in the 1960s, was made of ABS plastic. A departure from the drab workaday designs of office machines, it actually was conceived as a personal accessory, light and portable as a ballpoint pen, that could accommodate to any setting. *Photo: Olivetti*

to guess," stated the catalog, "at whether we are on the threshold of a 'Plastic Age,' but there are already many straws in the wind (plastic straws, of course) that would justify such a title. Our taste makes increasing demands for the qualities of lightness, immateriality, brilliant color and complex fluidity of form that can best be found in this continually growing gamut of chemical compounds."

In 1982, plastic production surpassed that of steel worldwide, and we formally entered the Plastic Age. The materials have become too pervasive to ignore and in many cases too complex to name. From the start plastics have been contradictory substances—mysterious in their elemental origins as organic chemicals, banal in their sheer ubiquity. In both industrial design and the decorative arts, the role of plastics has continually evolved from a mere substitute to that of an essential ingredient responsive both to human needs and fantasies.

1 VANITIES

34. A wire sheathed in blue Celluloid and studded with rhinestones forms an adjustable headband from the 1920s. *Fred Silberman; mannequin, Joia of Second Avenue*

Jewelry

If one word were needed to summon up the spirit of the twenties and thirties, "novelty" would do nicely. Everything was new, from cocktails to shortened hemlines, from attitudes to abstract art. Celluloid, Galalith, Aladdinite, and Bakelite were some of the romantic-sounding names for the new plastic materials that were being utilized, along with metals, glass, and semiprecious stones, in an entirely new merchandising category called "popular-priced jewelry novelties." This jewelry differed markedly, both in styling and spirit, from the "costume" jewelry produced during the 19th century, mostly in Birmingham, England, by Matthew Boulton. His factory had supplied a burgeoning middle class with attractive imitations in metal, glass, and semiprecious stones of traditional designs, worn with characteristic Victorian restraint. The carefree spirit of the postwar twenties dispensed with straitlaced Victorian ideas about personal adornment, including the minimal use of jewelry. Women now wore quantities of brace-

lets, all sorts of pins, "neck chains" (as necklaces were called), and trinkets in forms and styles dictated mostly by Parisian manufacturers. In 1921, an article in the *Notion and Novelty Review* remarked on the phenomenon: "In the days of our grandmothers, when to wear more than one or two bits of jewelry at a time was considered something that would only be done by what in those days were termed 'stage persons,' novelty jewelry as we know it today was a thing almost unheard of. The only ornaments or small pieces of jewelry worn by well-groomed women then were bits of jet fashioned into various shapes such as necklaces, earrings, brooches or bracelets, or else heavy jewelry made of engraved or chased gold or silver. The beautiful but light and strong types of jewelry grouped nowadays under the classification of 'novelty' or 'popular priced' jewelry would have been a revelation to our staid and dignified ancestors. . . ." Another article reported, "Imitation jewels are being so cleverly manufactured that in some cases it is very diffi-

35

35. A cluster of Celluloid bangles inlaid with colored rhinestones nestles in a serpentine upper-arm bracelet. Styling suggests the 1920s craze for diamondlike glitter and Egyptian motifs. *Richard Utilla*

36. The vogue for snake jewelry, popular during the Victorian period, enjoyed a revival in the 1920s. These two examples in Celluloid — a ruby-eyed bracelet and a hand-painted cigarette holder that can be worn like a finger ring—are unusual for their vivid coloring and detailing. *Richard Utilla*

36

cult to tell the difference between the imitation and the genuine article. Amber beads have been perfected both in color and appearance . . . so carefully that laid side by side with genuine amber the strings were indistinguishable. The imitation amber even responds to the amber test, that of attracting bits of paper lying under it." (See *Identifying Plastics*.)

Plastics would prove successful imitators of amber, horn, ivory, and tortoiseshell for years to come; but designers also began to indulge their fancies in the new spectrum that plastics offered. French blue, mottled green, yellow, purple, white, and shell were among the colors used in the Celluloid jewelry imported from Paris about 1919. These took the form of pendants and ornaments strung on ribbon or links carved to form an actual chain. "Galalith is in its heyday," reported the novelty trade in 1921, "and cut into queer shapes or combined with metal, it makes very attractive decorations. . . . many new bracelet forms are being introduced to complete the effect of the short sleeved gown. Some very popular styles are made of bakelith [sic] and galalith, set with rhinestones or colored settings."

Despite the infectious enthusiasm of the novelty manufacturers—the impression they created was of a universal phenomenon—jewelry produced in the new materials was at first purchased mainly by working-class women. Wealthy, chic women did not begin to warm to the idea until after 1925 when the French designer Coco Chanel introduced the radical notion of costume jewelry to couture. But even Chanel's

Hair Ornaments

The designs of combs, barrettes, and other ornaments, carved traditionally of tortoiseshell, horn, and ivory were easily adapted to softer Celluloid. Quantities of combs were made in America at Leominster, Massachusetts, and in Europe at Oyonnax, a small French village near the Swiss border. Both became major centers for plastics fabrication.

Although many women had bobbed their hair in the early twenties, longer hair was coming back into vogue by about 1925 in accordance with the Parisian dictum for *"des coiffures volumineuses."* Anchored in a chignon at the nape of the neck, large combs in mid-decade took on an Oriental look. They could be abstract, but many were naturalistic, such as giant butterflies that projected six to eight inches above the head. European women vacationing at fashionable spas reportedly were wearing dinner-plate-sized combs modeled on the monumental *peigne de luxe*, the mantilla combs worn by Andalusians for Holy Week or bullfights. *Photo of glitter-flecked comb, top: Celanese Plastics Division; rhinestone comb, Jacaranda*

37

38

37. A seven-inch-long belt buckle is remarkable for the delicacy and degree of openwork hand-carving. *Bill Smith*

38. This plastic bangle bracelet set with diamonds dates from the 1930s. The unlikely combination of materials suggests that the deisgn may have been a wealthy woman's whim. *Jane Van Nest*

mentioned. Still, the trend gradually took hold; and in *The Decorative Twenties*, Martin Battersby maintains that by 1925, "more and more women were taking to costume jewelry, both heavy in design and frankly artificial," and that about 1927 Chanel had introduced the idea of "sets of clips for hat and neckline."

In 1925, the modern style that we now call Art Deco—with its geometrics, zigzag motifs, and exotic influences—was introduced in Paris at the *Exposition des Art Decoratifs et Industrials Moderne*. Although the style was definitely new, owing little—as was its intent—to the past, materials and workmanship were in the most opulent tradition. Jewelry displayed at the Exposition, as designed by the leading jewelers of France, featured diamonds, platinum, oriental pearls, and colored gemstones. Without doubt, these sparkling treasures account for the heavy use of rhinestones in plastic jewelry of the period, especially for bangle bracelets and hair ornaments. A few prominent French designers of the twenties experimented with plastics, but their work is rarely signed. More often, high-style designs were reproduced in plastics and chrome that today seem sometimes more suited to the Deco style than the precious materials they copied. "Deco," it has been said, "was a style made for plastic." The workmanship found in this jewelry is often excellent, indicating perhaps a respect for the inherent beauty or appropriateness of the material.

With the onset of the worldwide Depression in 1929, the luxury markets, particularly for jewelry, were hard hit.

glass and metal replicas of her own very real personal jewels were in a sense opulent and not in quite the same class as the plastic novelties that were being produced at the time. (Chanel designed precious jewels as well, which were often copied—not necessarily in plastic—for the costume trade.) Fashion magazines such as *Vogue* rarely pictured costume jewelry, even of Chanel's type, until the late thirties, and even then plastics were rarely

Fine jewelry was more often seen being sold back to the fine jewelers along the rue de la Paix or Fifth Avenue by the "formerly opulent," as *Business Week* reported in 1931. Because of the low cost and novelty of its product, the plastics industry was one of the few to thrive during the Depression, and the jewelry business was one of its greatest successes. Women who recently had pawned their diamonds might be attracted now on a practical level to the colorful, inexpensive baubles that by the thirties had found their way into fine department stores. In the mid-thirties, *Plastics* magazine (later *Modern Plastics*) estimated that 40 to 50 percent of the jewelry sales in stores such as Saks, Bonwit's, and Miriam Haskel were plastic.

There were dozens of manufacturers of these wares, and in 1936 *Modern Plastics* sent a reporter to interview one of the first successful producers of plastic jewelry in America, George F. Berkander. His firm was located in Providence, Rhode Island, then and now one of the centers of the costume jewelry and novelty trade. As a young man, Berkander had been employed in Providence making decorative hair ornaments such as French-style combs and barrettes. Impressed with the ivory-like Celluloid vanity sets he saw displayed in a shop window, he was tempted to design jewelry out of the same material. Berkander had observed that women's hairstyles were changing and that soon there would be little demand for elaborate hair combs and barrette ornaments; so he began to experiment. His first piece was a small, plain bar pin, but he gradually devised

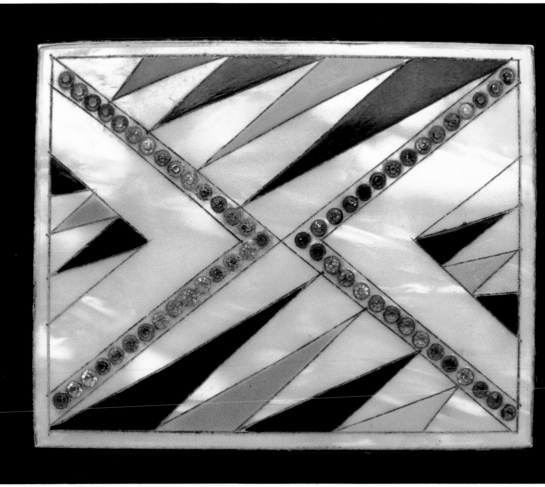

39

40

39. A belt buckle of pearlized Celluloid is hand-painted and inlaid with rhinestone zigzags typical of French Art Deco design from the 1920s. *Bill Smith*

40. Marked "Made in France," this bracelet was found in a London antique shop. It displays characteristic French elegance and careful workmanship although made of plastic. Onyx, lapis-lazuli, silver, and rose-cut diamonds are convincingly imitated. A circle of silvered metal at the base masks a breakaway clasp. *Bill Smith*

41

42

41. All-black jewelry provided women with a sophisticated alternative to bright colors in the 1930s. At top, a bracelet with a flexible plastic strap imitates Victorian jet. The one at center has a belt-buckle clasp. The ring has a single yellow stripe. *Top, Linda Campbell Franklin; center, Fred Silberman; bottom, author's collection*

42. Black plastic, enameled metal, and rhinestones are combined in this handsome Art Deco clip. About three inches long, it is solidly constructed, as the rear view shows, with a metal plate to which the plastic elements are screwed. *Bill Smith*

methods for setting pearls and rhinestones into the plastic, and, eventually, gold-plated design elements. Initially, Berkander had difficulty convincing buyers, especially men, that plastic jewelry was not a joke. But Henrietta Graff, the buyer for Berg Brothers on Lispenard Street in New York City, was persuaded to place a trial order for three gross. The article in *Modern Plastics* recounts that Miss Graff's orders found their way to Henry Siegal's department store on Sixth Avenue in New York where they were runaway bestsellers at about a dollar a piece. Within a short time, the items were being bought by jobbers for distribution throughout the country. Berkander said that by 1931 his company was producing inexpensive bracelets at the rate of more than a thousand gross a day, for which three tons of plastic materials a day were used on one item alone. He also made novelties and party goods, as well as an occasional "custom" piece such as Celluloid elephant chains for the wives of Presidents Harding and Coolidge; and tiny Celluloid airplanes with Lindbergh's name on them were ready for sale when the flyer landed in Paris in May, 1927. Berkander took credit for devising the first cellulose-acetate flower pins, which found appreciative buyers in the fine Fifth Avenue department stores. He was proud of his design staff, who, he said, were graduates of art schools. Their designs, he reported, were frequently copied in Paris—the ultimate form of flattery—and in Japan, where once copied they were exported to the U.S. and sold at one-third of the original price. By the late twenties, Berkander had several major competitors, not only in New England but in New York where the big producers of phenolic resin novelties, such as Catalin and Marblette, were located. The jewelry produced by these companies was bold and colorful, in dramatic contrast to earlier, delicate Celluloid. Bracelets, pins, and clips were typically chunky, a result of the way in which the resin was processed.

Phenolic resins used in jewelry were cast as rods, tubes, and slabs that were then sliced into individual pieces, or blanks, which were worked by operators seated at semiautomatic lathes and drills. It was not exactly an assemblyline operation, because each worker completed a piece entirely on his own. Bracelets and rings were sawed from tubes and "carved" by the operator, who, much like a glass etcher, would hold the surface against the lathe to create a pattern. Because of the good heat resistance of phenolics, the pieces could withstand the friction of the wheels without melting or getting gummy. The designs followed trends—florals and geometrics are perhaps the most numerous. However, it is difficult today to find any two exactly alike. Pins, lapel clips, and buckles were cut from patterns by means of a jigsaw and then lathe-carved; or they might be sliced from 24- to 30-inch long sections that had been molded in a particular cross-section profile—a butterfly, for example—so that when sliced the rod could provide many duplicates with the same shape.

The cleanliness of these plants, and presumably the health of the operators who sat at the grinding wheels day after day, was evidently a concern of some manufacturers. A reporter from *Modern Plastics* visiting Ace Plastics in Long Island City in 1936 described the scene on the factory floor, where dozens of men seated at rows of worktables toiled all day. Each wheel "was equipped with a small powerful suction tube with a funnel-shaped opening which sucks up all waste material as it is ground by the wheel and removes it from the building leaving hardly a speck of dust on the workman's bench and absolutely none in the air of the room."

As operators completed batches of jewelry, the pieces were taken to be

43. French necklaces from the 1920s and '30s include, at left, a chrome snake choker tipped in plastic; center, a coral, black, and chrome choker with perfectly fitted links. On the right, the stepped design is created by means of ingeniously pieced construction. The red and black sections that form the pendant are engraved with the signature of the designer, August Bonaz. *Primavera Gallery*

44. A cuff bracelet, one of a pair designed in France in the 1920s by August Bonaz, is made of the casein plastic Galalith. Masterfully carved and fitted, each two-colored longitudinal segment is one piece. The whole is held together by elastic at top and bottom. *Primavera Gallery*

45. These typical English pendant necklaces of the 1930s are made of chrome-plated metal and casein plastic in tones of jade and carnelian. *Richard Utilla*

46. Unusual shapes and arrangements of beads and pendants, plus strong Art Deco styling, suggest possible French design of these chrome and plastic necklaces. *Fred Silberman*

47. The unknown designer of this elasticized cuff bracelet from the 1930s achieved elegant proportions by using yellow rods and metal beads as spacers between chunky green segments. *Susan Ellsworth*

polished in revolving tumblers, big maple-lined steel drums filled with sawdust and wooden pegs that removed surface scratches. Deeply carved pieces, however, were often "ashed," a process that involved rubbing a piece with wet pumice on muslin wheels that could smooth the deep recesses. The pumice was then washed off and the pieces polished on dry muslin wheels. Metal findings such as clasps and pin backs were added in the final stage by women using foot-operated presses. This was for the simplest type of jewelry, which did not require piecing or stringing, inlay, plating, or, in some cases, hand-painting. All of these time-consuming hand operations kept cast phenolic in the upper price brackets well into the 1940s. Cheaper dime-store jewelry was more often injection-molded and flimsy.

Several techniques were developed for combining metals with plastics to impart a more legitimate look of "real" jewelry. Strips of gilded or silvered metal would be hand-wrapped, fitted into grooves, or attached with tiny screws. By the mid-thirties, a method was developed, probably in France, for pouring molten metal into precut channels. An article in a 1936 issue of *Notion and Novelty Review* explained how this was done. A metal was first devised that could be poured at lukewarm temperature, so as not to char the

45

46

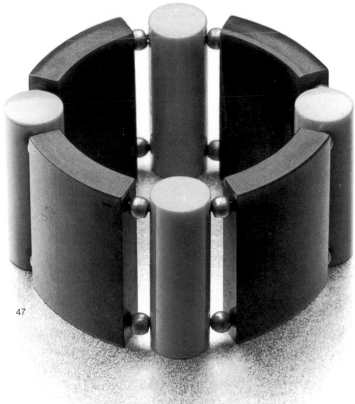

47

plastic. It was then applied in any one of three ways. First it might be poured into shallow surface grooves, about 1/16th of an inch deep, after which the surface was polished and smoothed. Second, holes might be bored through the plastic in a decorative pattern and the metal poured to fill them. Finally, an intricate pattern might be jigsawed through the plastic and the space filled with the molten metal. This technique was used widely on buttons, buckles, and dress clips, but, judging from the rarity of examples, it must have proved very costly and time-consuming.

The plating of entire pieces of plastic was attempted before 1910, but the fairly complicated electrolytic process required for coating complex shapes was not common until the forties. Even then, the process was extremely time-consuming and needed refinement, which came about after the war. In the early plating efforts, the surface of a die-pressed article was coated with varnish and, while still tacky, sprayed with a conducting agent. It was then immersed in an acid bronze stop bath in order to obtain a metallized surface that other metals such as 14K gold or copper would adhere to. The final metallizing was obtained by placing the piece in an electrolytic bath. When dry, the surface was polished to even the plating, and a final coat of lacquer added a high gloss. In the 1950s, improved techniques made it possible to plate plastics easily with a shiny metal finish—for better or worse—that did not require hand-polishing. It was applied not only to jewelry but all types of accessories, even automobile ornaments, and quite appropriately to plas-

49

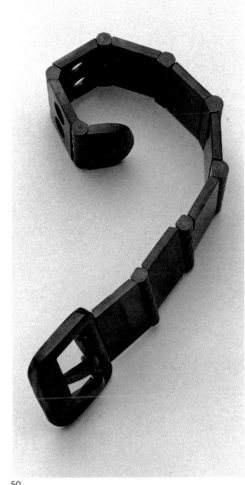

50

tic film to make sequins.

Plastics were often inset with other plastics of contrasting color. In the higher-priced jewelry, cast plastics were molded to resemble hand-cut stones, and the "stones" were then usually set into bracelets. Plastics were also combined with wood, although rarely (before the craft revival of the seventies) with precious metals and stones. Notable early exceptions include the Trifari pins on page 57 and the bracelet on page 40 that has been set with diamonds.

As previously noted, the high fashion magazines devoted very little space to costume jewelry; and during the Depression even the trade publications of the notions and novelties industry dropped coverage of the jewelry markets to concentrate on home-sewing aids and equipment. This left *Modern Plastics* as the most unlikely but most conscientious reporter in the field.

48. Elsa Schiaparelli designed this bizarre necklace in the 1930s, using a strip of flexible vinyl to which multicolored metal insects were applied. *Photo: Brooklyn Museum, Millicent Rogers Collection*

49. Links formed of compressed plastic "crystals" to simulate amberoid alternate with enamelled metal in this elasticized bracelet made in France in the 1930s. *Fred Silberman*

50. A bracelet of marbleized green plastic links is strung on elastic and fastens like a belt. *Bill Smith*

52

53

51. Chunky bracelets like these were produced by the hundreds of thousands in the 1930s. "Blanks" were first sliced from tubes of cast phenolic resin, then individually "carved" on lathes and tumble-polished like gemstones. *Susan Ellsworth*

52. Cubist clips flank a streamlined belt buckle, all from the 1930s. *Author's collection*

53. Although not found together, this bracelet and ring may originally have been designed as a set in the 1930s. *Fred Silberman*

54. This carved buckle, clip, and pin display the subtle coloring possible with Depression-era plastics. *Author's collection*

54

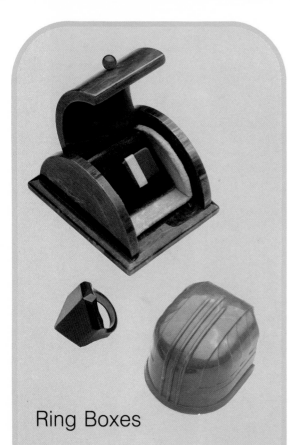

Ring Boxes

Women who married during the Depression often recall receiving their engagement and wedding rings in colorful, streamlined plastic boxes like these. The marbleized colors chosen to imitate semi-precious stones such as jade and rose quartz were considered elegant enough for conveying precious jewels such as diamonds and gold. But rarely, if ever, were inexpensive plastic rings—made from the same cast phenolic resin—delivered in them. Indeed, plastic rings are often too large and chunky to fit comfortably inside these satin-lined boxes, which are today fairly rare. Though realized on a small scale, they remain some of the best examples of the new packaging concepts introduced during the thirties, in which color and molded forms were the prerequisites. *Carol Ferranti*

55

Some of the magazine's coverage came from the Du Pont Style Service in Paris, which regularly supplied industry publications with news on trends and designs on the Continent. In 1931, for example, the service reported that "Pyroxylin (Celluloid) was the new material used for boudoir accessories and jewelry . . . rings, necklaces, bracelets. New models by Blanchet are made of transparent composition with encrusted motifs in jade, green, turquoise, blue and black." Crude sketches accompanying these bulletins might show chunky bangles decorated with oversized, metal monogram letters, huge translucent beads strung on elastic, or white plastic set with metal rings. In 1937, the "Plastic Modes" column of *Modern Plastics* ran sketches of Chanel's oversized translucent plastic eyeglasses and black scalloped buttons, both studded with rhinestones. Worth was represented with a handbag and matching vest covered with black, amber, and yellow cellulose spangles (sequins) and a Sphinx brooch of colored plastic with gold

55. Oversized, toylike pins were produced in America during the 1940s. The four-inch-long airplane with spinnable propeller is composed of four hand-carved parts. The heart, pierced by eight small hearts, is remarkably clean and undamaged considering its age. Both are rare and made of cast phenolic resin. *Susan Ellsworth*

56. Eight life-sized cherries make up this lapel pin from the 1940s—rare for its size and mint condition. *Susan Ellsworth*

57

58

59

57. Metal added realistic touches and sparkle to plastic jewelry. However, the handwork required to affix chains, studs, and banding to pins like this horse and saber increased their cost. *Susan Ellsworth*

58. Lapel pins in the form of picture hats come in many charming variants. This 2½ inch example has hand-painted polka dots and a fabric band. *Douglas Taylor*

59. Puppetlike pins such as these three-inch examples are hard to find with no missing parts. These are hand-painted and resemble crib toys of the period. *Douglas Taylor*

metal and rhinestones (proving that Egyptian motifs continued to be popular well after the twenties craze that was sparked by the opening of King Tut's tomb in 1922). Goupy actually showed plastic evening jewelry—large, solid cuff bracelets set with stones and a matching belt buckle—to complement a lace gown. Hermes, a firm known primarily for leather luxury goods, experimented with plastic in the late-thirties to create a bracelet watch decorated in black enamel set into colored plastic, and a traveling watch with plastic molding in a pigskin case. Cartier used plastic, generally acrylic, as buckles on evening bags and in one case designed a wristwatch with a Bakelite case (page 56).

In the late-thirties, Elsa Schiaparelli, a designer noted for her innovative and often surrealistic approach to fashion—largely inspired by her friend Salvador Dali—began to use plastics in accessories. These included buttons (pages 65–67) but also jewelry and trimmings. One of her most bizarre pieces of jewelry—of those on record—is the vinyl collar (page 46) imbedded with multicolored metal insects, mostly beetles and dragonflies. She also designed an ice-cube necklace of pink and crystal plastic cubes and unusual belt clasps, one with a pair of hands with painted fingernails. In her autobiography, *Shocking Life*, she refers to "our own unusual jewelry of enameled ivy necklaces [that] went like lightning as did the first Plexiglass bracelets and earrings. They were designed by men of extraordinary talent [such as] Jean Clement, a genius in his way, a real French artisan." Unfortunately, as with so many designs of the period, visual records of these pieces are hard to find.

The same may be said for the jewelry itself, intriguingly described by Martin Battersby in *The Decorative Thirties* as "barbaric." Inspired by the Colonial Exhibition of 1931, the jewelry was made, he says, of "gilded or silvered metal combined with enamelling carved from horn . . . tortoiseshell or artificial substances like galalith and catalin, the forms being drawn from Negro prototypes and blended with cubism." Battersby provides a sketch of a bracelet by the prominent designer Jean Fouquet that he feels demonstrates the "avant-garde obsession with machinery." It is made of ebonite (vulcanized rubber) rings enclosing chromium-plated ball-bearings, the heads of the connection screws being left unconcealed.

American Styles

What American jewelry may have lacked in such hard chic, it often made up for in humor and childlike imagery. Lapel pins such as the giant heart and the airplane on page 50 illustrated the trend to almost toylike designs that were produced in America. Pins molded as picture hats, dancing puppets, clothespins, all types of animals and sea life are among the most desirable pieces today and are rarer than the

60. Plastics often imitated Victorian forms with more or less success. Here a chunky "cameo" is created simply by gluing a stamped image made from cellulose acetate onto a phenolic slab—incongruous and kitschy. The iridescent Celluloid heart, on the other hand, is a more pleasing match of form and material. *Author's collection*

60

61. Small lapel pins in two popular motifs are rendered here in different plastics and methods. The c. 1940s palm tree, about two inches high, is injection molded—a mass-production technique— probably of cellulose acetate. The c. 1930 carved hand, reminiscent of 19th-century folk art, is made of phenolic resin. *Carol Ferranti*

62. Flower cluster necklaces made of cellulose acetate were typical of American dime-store jewelry during the 1940s, when they sold for about a dollar apiece. Necklace chains hung with abstract decorations were also common, but the combination of wood and plastic, as in the carved leaf and berry choker at left, is more unusual. *Susan Ellsworth; author's collection*

61

62

more conventional floral and geometric motifs, especially in very large sizes. Themes, sets, or coordinated designs were popular, as this fashion note from 1936 illustrates: "Frances Stevens, radio songbird, pins back her modified sombrero with a forbidding six-shooter in grey cast resin. On her silk scarf she pins a matching miniature ten-gallon Stetson with bright red band."

In the same year, the Catalin Corporation ran a full-page color advertisement for "deliciously tempting 'style fruits' carved of Catalin for 'costume adornment,'" adding that the line also included pickles and carrots. Fabricators could purchase these forms and turn them into pins, clips, or buttons simply by attaching the appropriate hardware.

Ever pursuing the ultimate merchandising angle, fabricators would vary their jewelry lines by color to accommodate seasonal clothing styles and produced, for example, dark browns, black, carnelian, and greens for fall and winter tweeds. In 1935, the regency costumes in Noel Coward's play *Con-*

63. Acrylic jewelry—faceted, engraved, molded, and carved like crystal—was first designed and produced in Germany in the late 1930s. These examples are made of Plexiglas, the acrylic resin developed by the Rohm & Haas Company. *Photo: Rohm & Haas*

Time Plastic

Both luxurious and inexpensive watches sported plastic cases during the Depression. A women's wristwatch, left, made and signed by Cartier, has a black Bakelite and yellow gold case, a white enamel dial, and a black suede strap. It sold at auction in 1982 for $4,400. The handbag watch, designed by DeVaulchier & Blow for Westclox, was included in the 1934 "Machine Art" exhibition at the Museum of Modern Art. The case was produced in black Bakelite and, as shown, with a white lacquer finish. *Photo of Cartier watch: Christie's, New York; handbag watch: Richard Utilla*

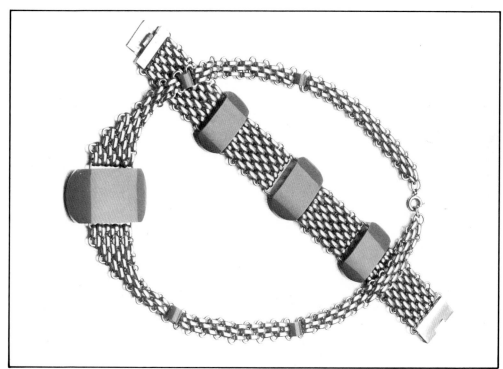

64

65

versation Piece supposedly inspired a vogue for pastels that plastic jewelry manufacturers were quick to capitalize on.

In the fall of 1940, plastics figured in a special wartime collection of jewelry promoted by Lord & Taylor to benefit Mme. Chiang Kai-shek's war-orphans fund. The store offered American adaptations, in gilt metal and plastic, of antique Chinese jewelry, with a royalty for the sale of each piece going to the fund. The designs incorporated plastic reproductions of Chinese carved medallions in jade, carnelian, and lapis lazuli. In England, in 1941, another wartime promotion featured Lucky Bracelets, simple bangles priced at the equivalent of $1.00 each ("worn by the Duchess of Kent") made from acrylic offcuts used in the manufacture of bulletproof windscreens for Spitfire and Hurricane fighter-planes.

The wartime dearth of all types of luxury goods turned many more women toward costume jewelry, which unfortunately began to lose much of its distinctive styling—the chic Deco motifs

64–65. Well-made costume jewelry from the 1940s was often of metal and plastic combinations. The German-made set, above, pairs chrome mesh with teal blue plastic. The choker, below, has injection-molded plastic inserts in gilt metal links. *Fred Silberman; Mary C. Oppido*

66. Pins by Trifari from the 1950s utilize molded acrylic, sterling silver, and marcasite. The frog's eyes are colored glass. *Fred Silberman*

67

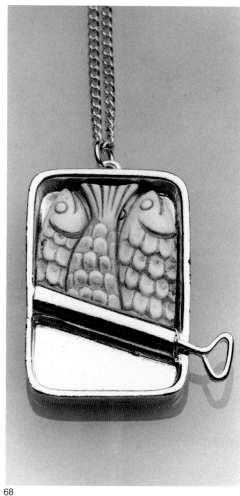

68

67. Art jewelry from the 1960s sometimes resembled body armor, like this acrylic breastplate designed by Carolyn Kriegman in 1969. *Photo: Lee Nordness*

68. A humorous two-inch-long pendant marked "Hatti Carnegie" dates from the late 1960s, when the firm produced several lines of Pop Art jewelry items. The fish in the chrome-plated can are molded plastic. *Author's collection*

69

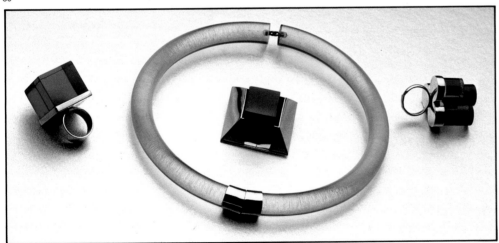

70

69. Chanel-style ropes of beads on gold-plated chain are typical of the quality costume jewelry made during the 1950s. The German-made chain at top features large acrylic beads spaced along contoured, textured links. Below, the small-faceted acrylic beads act as spacers between the larger satin-finished balls. *Anne DiNoto; Marie d'Elia*

70. Supercool designs in hand-dyed acrylic and chrome by Bill Smith date from the late 1950s and early '60s. The pull-apart pink choker fastens in front with a magnetic clasp. The brooch and rings feature massive acrylic "jewels" that suggest cosmic crystals. *Bill Smith*

71. Stanley Lechtzin, an American jewelry designer noted for his work with plastics and metal, created this Cameo Corsage in 1979 using cast acrylic, electroformed silver and gilt, and pearls. Measuring 6 x 4 x 3 inches, the piece fulfills the designer's definition of jewelry as not only "an art form with the function of embellishing the body" but also as "something that can be appreciated in isolation."
Photo: Stanley Lechtzin

72. Artist-craftsman Bob Natalini used cast polyester resin to form the housing for this unusual pendant that encapsulates a tropical beetle and functioning electronics. *Photo: Bob Natalini*

71

and exaggerated whimsy that make the prewar period so attractive to collectors. During the forties, there was a considerable increase in the use of gilt metal with plastics and a reversion to conventionalized designs in an attempt to create an "antique" look in the form of teardrop pendants and floral sprays. In such designs, glass would have been the preferred material since, in gilt settings, it suggested the glitter of real stones a bit more convincingly. However, when the war in Europe cut off America's supplies of glass imported from Czechoslovakia—upon which the bustling costume jewelry industry had depended heavily—American manufacturers attempted to find substitutes with various types of resins. Acrylic, molded as gemstones or carved to resemble rock crystal, was adopted following the examples of German acrylic imports of the thirties. But one of the oddest, short-lived American experiments was the introduction of "Coltstones," made of molded phenolic resin (Bakelite) by

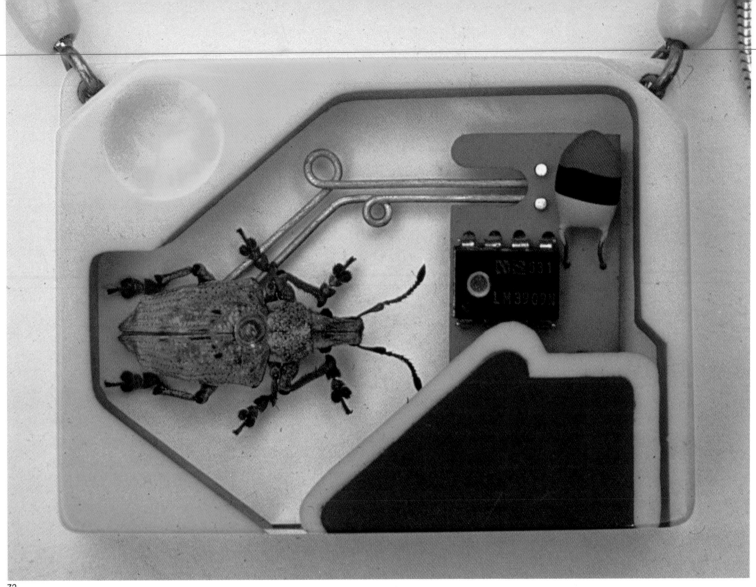

the plastics division of the Colt's Patent Firearms Manufacturing Company. The "stones" came in a range of background colors flecked with contrasting particles. Colt promoted them, not too successfully, for women's jewelry and men's cufflinks, tie pins, and the like. Examples are rare today.

Immediately after the war, jewelry sales in every category boomed. In 1946, *Business Week* explained that "wartime boosts in revenue have driven

jewelry sales (highly sensitive to disposable income) steadily uphill. In five years the jewelry business has tripled, against an approximate doubling of all retail sales." The editors were talking about the sales of fine jewelry, which in 1931 had bottomed out. But fifteen years later, the picture had begun to change. The costume jewelry market, which had done well during the Depression, now gathered increased momentum, too. *Business Week* noted

that "aside from the increased income, jewelry has also been favored for its availability, its usefulness in smartening old clothes."

In England, jewelry was displayed with all types of consumer goods at the "Britain Can Make It Exhibition" of 1946 in London. In the catalog, Arnold Selwyn noted that insofar as precious metals were used, the styles tended to remain conservative ("for it has to be remembered that the more modish an article is, the sooner it is outmoded"). They exhibited a "floral tendency" as "a reaction against the formalism, the geometrical rectitude, that marked the previous phase . . . a deliberate avoidance of mechanical orderliness." Plastic brooches and earclips in contrasting tones, shown in colors such as cream or coral, or rose-pink and a deeper red were popular, as were imitation Victorian cameos bearing a woman's head. The catalog displayed, along with dia-

mond watches and other fine pieces, an elegant necklace of acrylic beads combined with gilt metal.

The Pop-It Decade

In America, the fifties produced very little in the way of inspired plastic jewelry design unless you count the erstwhile Pop-It bead, now relegated to the fifty-cent box at thrift shops. It seemed like a good idea at the time, and in many ways it symbolized the spirit of

conformity that pervaded the early 1950s. Each bead with its plug-and-socket construction could be endlessly attached to others like it. But the mini-module was produced in bland, unattractive colors—such as frosted pastels—and with variation in size but not shape. Ultimately, the toylike Pop-Its were more fun to pop and unpop than wear. (Today the idea has in fact been resurrected as a toy—giant plastic beads for infants to pull apart and

73

74

73. Delicately hand-tinted acrylic wedges double-strung on silk cord make up this contemporary necklace by Christopher Walling. When worn, it drapes around the neck to form a square collar. *Christopher Walling*

74. The sunburst pattern of this acrylic bracelet was cut in France with a laser in 1976 after a design by Tabakof. *Author's collection*

75. Ivy Ross created jewelry ensembles with Color-core plastic laminate and silver to complement her hand-knitted clothing designs. *Photo: Ivy Ross*

76. Hi-tech jewelry designs by Suzanne Bachner are made of Formica brand laminate. *Photo: Tomo; Formica*

75

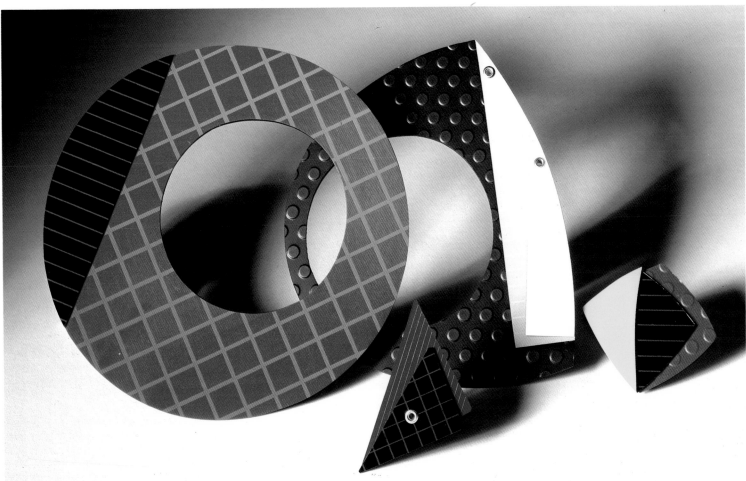

76

reattach.) Why the designer never thought to create more interesting bead forms, such as geometrics or realistics, is a mystery, but this probably was due to the high cost of dies for injection molding and the generally conservative approach to accessories during that period. The ho-hum elegance of gold circle pins, a revival of Chanel's nicely gaudy chains, cultured and "good" imitation pearls (plastic-based in most cases), and "good" imitations of fine jewelry by firms such as Monet, Trifari, and Ciro prevailed until Sputnik, the first orbiting satellite, ushered in the Space Age in 1957.

The emerging space technology entranced designers who saw a new romantic imagery in the functional, "far out," unpretty motifs of common hardware. Plastics, particularly transparent acrylic, imparted an ethereal quality to hard-edged design. In 1958, for example, designer Bill Smith created a rigid acrylic necklace with magnet catch (page 59), a square acrylic bracelet with chrome elbow-joint pipe corners, and oversized space-jewel rings in limited numbers for boutique sales.

Craft Jewelry

Boutiques offered costume jewelry designers an outlet for experimental pieces that, because of concept or degree of handwork necessary, were not ideally suited to the demands and requirements of mass-production. This commercial trend complemented the craft revival of the late sixties, particularly the renewed interest in art jewelry that sparked experimentation with synthetics and other industrial materials.

Many craftspeople preferred acrylic in the form of rod, sheet, or tube because it is so easily cut, sliced, or lathe-turned without specialized tools. But in the seventies, artists such as Stanley Lechtzin and Bob Natalini developed more sophisticated techniques for working directly with cast resins—polyester, acrylic, and epoxies—in combination with metals such as gold, silver, titanium, aluminum, and brass. In the eighties, designers Ivy Ross and Suzanne Bachner began to fabricate jewelry from thin sheets of decorative laminate such as Formica's Colorcore pastels and a range of high-tech patterns.

In a 1969 interview with *Women's Wear Daily*, the art dealer Lee Nordness commented that the young artists who made craft jewelry "usually sell their wares through word of mouth or at country fairs or in a few galleries outside of New York." By the early eighties, that situation had changed only a little. Today one can find unique items in department store boutiques as well as in specialized craft and art jewelry shops. But the virtuosity of the artists working in plastics has increased impressively, as have the prices, which could easily range from several hundred to several thousand for single items. In most cases, pieces are signed and sometimes dated, important and desirable additions to any artwork, especially if one is concerned with the investment value of objects.

Buttons

Buttons are the accessory most closely related to jewelry. Although they have been produced in every technique and material known to the decorative arts, plastic examples are no less fascinating than those made of more precious substances. Plastic buttons can be miniature exercises in abstract art or amusing realistic representations of everything from pickles to top hats. In the pre-plastic era, most buttons were made of mother-of-pearl derived from South Sea oyster shell and native American mollusk shell. Before 1914, the United States imported most of its buttons from Europe—primarily England and Germany—but with the onset of the first World War these foreign ports were closed, forcing the American button business not only to shift its trade to Japan and the Philippines but to develop its own industry in order to supply the demands of the armed forces during the war. By 1919, the *Notion and Novelty Review* reported that American exports were 86 percent greater than imports, a reversal of the prewar situation. At that time, the most valuable buttons (excepting those of precious materials) were ocean pearl shell, followed by freshwater pearl, then vegetable ivory (from the South American tagua nut). After that came "covered, Celluloid, shoe, bone, and horn." The price of Celluloid was still high at that time, because of the wartime shortages of raw materials.

As with jewelry, Celluloid and casein plastics were used extensively for buttons until the early 1930s when cast phenolic resin became the preferred material. It could be carved and inset with other materials, and thus generally provided a bolder, more colorful and dramatic accent than had been available previously. Button wearing in the thirties and forties was, by today's

77

77. Button collectors refer to these 1930s plastics formed in realistic shapes, quite logically, as "realistics." As a category, they are rare and scarce today. Of those shown at left, examples that display intricate hand-carving, such as the blackbird, or painting, such as the boot, are most valuable.
Tender Buttons

and made plastic buttons for her famous nipped-waist suits of clown heads, acrobats, and horses; but also lacquer red lips, paperweights, hand mirrors, whisk brooms, decanters, chessmen, electric light bulbs, and boxing gloves. In her autobiography she says, "In spite of the zipper [she introduced the zipper—and synthetic fabric—to couture] King Button reigned without fear at Schiaparelli's . . . but not one looked like what a button was supposed to look like." Her fellow designers in Paris made an attempt to do likewise. In 1936, the *Notion and Novelty Review* reported from Paris that Marcel Rochas had made cathedral window buttons of carved Catalin painted to look like stained glass and Jacques Heim was featuring black plastic top hat buttons for simple afternoon dresses. Not to be outdone, the New York firm Harlem Adler offered plastic bathtub stopper buttons, complete with little metal rings "with which to pull them out." (Schiaparelli probably inspired

standards, profligate. Buttons found a place on cuffs, pockets, shoulders, at the waist, on the belt, even on garters; and, in 1949, Schiaparelli designed a bathing suit with a row of buttons up the side. Schiaparelli can, in fact, be credited with instigating much of the buttonmania of the thirties. Her famous snug evening jackets—each an artful custom design usually in crepe or velvet—were regularly bedecked with all types of trimmings, including gold braid and sequins, glass and tiny plastic flowers. But always her passion for oversized and unusual buttons would be apparent. Schiaparelli's well-known sense of humor inspired her to create fanciful and amusing buttons for often surrealistic clothing designs and inspired the big button manufacturers, such as B. Blumenthal, Schwanda, and the Lidz Brothers in New York, to manufacture novel designs for the high fashion market. She loved circus imagery

78. A wealth of rare plastic buttons is assembled here, in classic collector fashion, as "boards." The largest button measures two inches in diameter. Hand-carving, faceting, and metal inlay are among the many techniques used to create complex abstract patterns and shapes. *Tender Buttons*

Hollywood costume designer Orry-Kelly, who created a sheer silk jersey blouse secured by three baby-sized fist-buttons for Ann Sheridan in *The Man Who Came to Dinner* in 1942.)

In 1939, the *New York Journal-American* showed a fall suit from Lord & Taylor fitted with a row of Celluloid buttons shaped like little cakes in square, fluted pans textured to look like leather(!) "in three sizes and excellent fall colors." In the accompanying article, the writer remarked that button fashions changed quickly and that button designers "suffer more than most people in the pangs of creation. There have been so many kinds of buttons, it's hard to find a fresh idea." This accounts for the rarity of novelty buttons today, especially the realistics, like the cake pans, that were a quickly passing fad. Also, these buttons were not injection-molded by the thousands as most buttons are today.

Apart from the realistics, the most magnificent and artistic buttons of the thirties are large, abstract, sometimes architectural designs created for use on heavy coat and suit fabric. These can range to two or more inches in diameter and are often formed as spirals, circles, cylinders, and pyramids. Layers of colored plastic are often inlaid with contrasting colors or combined with wood or metal to produce striking designs often reminiscent of machine parts or rational forms inspired by machinery. Whether this imagery was conscious or accidental is hard to say, but the trend is reflected in other areas—such as textile motifs and, of course, abstract art such as the exuberant paintings and murals of Sonia and Robert Delaunay. The colorful segmented discs of color that appear in their work could easily have inspired button design of the period, or vice versa.

During World War II, buttons also served sometimes as more than fasteners. In England during the blackouts, it was common to carry or wear something white, or wear a luminous button on the lapel. In America, "V for Victory" appeared as a button motif. And in what may have been an effort to boost sales, the Buick automobile company initiated a tie-in with La Mode Buttons for a special promotion called the "auto motif fashion group." Plastic buttons were designed bearing the Buick motifs of fireball engine (a comet), the corporate shield, the radiator grillework, and the stylized draped figure of the "Goddess of Speed." In addition, the ensemble included a woman's belt buckle in the form of a near actual-size "license plate" bearing the numbers "1941." It is doubtful that this promotion, which also involved the manufacturers of fabric and women's and children's wear, ever got off the ground; but it certainly attests to the perceived power of a button outside of the fashion community.

It is probable that the increased use of acrylic buttons during and after the war was the result of the button industry's use of scrap and off-cuts obtained from the government, where the material was used for bomber gun turrets. Before the war, of course, acrylic already had been used as a crystal substitute and, as we have seen, for making jewelry in Germany. The transparency and sparkle of acrylic suited the postwar taste for less bold and more "feminine" styling. The result was an increase in the use of flower motifs, also much in favor for jewelry. But these have none of the strikingly graphic appeal of the realistics and geometrics of the thirties. However, in 1946, one maker produced undercut Lucite fish bowls, complete with fish and bubbles, that would be a treasure to find today. In mid-1947, La Mode, a division of B. Blumenthal, produced a line of realistics, aimed at teens, designed by Marian Weeber in the shapes of dress forms, pin cushions, spools of thread, and such. These were reminiscent of a line of "Blackboard Buttons" styled for schoolkids ten years earlier, with designs etched in white on a black background of children's drawings. But the era of amusing figurative buttons for use by fashionable women was pretty much over.

The fifties and sixties saw a decline in button design. Colors became increasingly garish and designs more and more conventional. A notable ex-

79

ception occurred in the 1970s when a technique was developed for laminating fabric and ribbon in plastic that produced charming results; and by the eighties, couturière plastic buttons were once again being produced in Europe, suggesting the distinct possibility of a button renaissance.

Fashion Accessories

Just as plastic buttons sprouted on clothing, plastic accessories began to appear in the form of oversized eyeglass frames, umbrella handles, handbag clasps, belts (sometimes handpainted and jeweled), and outlandish trimmings for hats, as well as in the shoe trade in the form of transparent heels and uppers. At the Paris International Exhibition of 1938, cellulose acetate plastics were displayed in many forms and categories, and *Modern Plastics* magazine reported that the most interesting developments in the fashion field included: ". . . plastic hats by Agnes, glass [probably a

form of cellophane] fabrics and cellulose [rayon] scarfs by Colcombet, spangled dresses, mules and shoes with transparent cellulose acetate tops, and decorative flowers in fluorescent material or perliane."

Enthusiasm for plastic materials in fashion—including synthetic fabric— would wax and wane over the ensuing decades, of course; but initially, as in other areas, just the existence of these new materials was cause for comment.

Shoes

Soft flexible vinyl sheeting was first used in shoes in the late thirties. Saks Fifth Avenue was one of the first luxury department stores to carry dressy sandals that combined vinyl with suede and kid for the "Cinderella slipper" effect that was to become very popular in the fifties. Many women loved the idea of see-through shoes and found vinyl comfortable as long as it was perforated to allow the foot to breathe. In the fifties, designers such as Seymour Troy and Stanley Philipson combined vinyl with spike heels and sling backs for sexy and delicate shoes that were sometimes handpainted or otherwise decorated with glitter and foil. In cheaper versions, acrylic heels or wedges were often molded to encapsulate flowers and novelties (dice and aquaria, for example). Despite their considerable weight, acrylic soles were sometimes built up to extravagant and precarious heights and filled with glitter as mod fashions of the sixties dictated.

In the late sixties and seventies, American designers Beth and Herbert Levine reintroduced the idea of vinyl to the fine shoe market but included sporty as well as dressy styles in their collection. The Levines created a clear vinyl loafer with low walking heel as well as sleek pumps with crystal-clear high heels. Their method for affixing the transparent heel to the last without nails, which are usually visible, gave their shoes an added elegance. The Levines also invented the stretch vinyl boot, which was widely copied.

While the Levines and other designers used vinyl in sheet form much as traditional shoemakers used leather, one contemporary designer—Joe Famolare—made innovative use of molding technology to produce a polyurethane clog in the early eighties. Famolare turned to molding in an effort to produce the traditional Scandinavian form as inexpensively as possible. The result (this page) was achieved by using expanding polyurethane foam in a two-stage rotary mold with multiple dies that could produce thousands a

82

83

81–83. The inventive shoe designs on these pages are all by Beth Levine, a designer who is noted for creative use of plastics. The assortment on the facing page combines vinyl and acrylic with leather and satin. The Pop Art racing car shoe from the 1960s, left, is basically a patent leather loafer transformed by a vinyl windscreen and wheel appliques. The glittering mule, custom made for the designer Michael Vollbracht, has a carved acrylic wedge and mesh upper embroidered with crystal beads. *Beth Levine; Michael Vollbracht*

and acrylic clasps and handles out of the thirties resemble the jewelry fashioned from the same material. But designers of the thirties were inventive at discovering additional ways to ornament and otherwise form purses from the new plastics. Fabric bags were decorated with tight coils of extruded cellulose acetate and with plastic flowers. And during the Depression, kits were sold containing injection-molded plastic tiles, perforated at the corners, that could be linked or sewed together to make zippered clutch bags. Lightweight and colorful with a chainmail effect, these bags—now standard flea-market items—were as futuristic in their time as Paco Rabanne's disc dresses in the sixties (page 76). When, in the fifties, manufacturers adopted acrylic for the creation of rigid dress bags, the results were on the one hand gaudy (or vulgar, or amusing, depending on your point of view) or stylish on the other when handled with restraint. In either case, the rigid bag was a fad that was

day. In the process, each clog is first molded then ejected and washed with detergent to remove the color- and adhesive-resistant patina that forms naturally during molding. After drying, the clog is dipped in color baths and buffed to achieve shaded, woodlike effects, or sprayed if a multicolored effect is desired. The result, which is comfortable, sturdy, waterproof, and cheap (retailing for about $10.00) would be appropriate, according to the

designer, "if one were going to design a shoe for a nation."

Handbags

Plastic clasps for handbags can be found on beaded purses from the twenties, a period when Celluloid and casein plastics were most common. These can be as delicate in appearance as the "ivory" and "tortoiseshell" jewelry and vanity items from the same period. Likewise, the chunky phenolic

84. Judith Leiber's molded Lucite evening bag, sparkling with rhinestones and made in the 1970s, demonstrates the degree of glamor and elegance achievable with plastics. *Judith Leiber*

85. This evening bag of smoky gray acrylic, c. 1940, could be mistaken for a camera case. *Anne DiNoto*

generally uncomfortable to carry, with its hard plastic handle, and noisy, with its contents clattering around inside. They are collected today more as kitsch sculpture than fashion. Exceptional examples achieve elegance, however, when the molded form is understated or when applied decoration displays the finesse of, say, Judith Leiber's evening bag from the seventies (below). Among the wittiest of plastic designs from that period are the vinyl clutch bags printed to look exactly like a rolled-up magazine.

Eyeglasses

Plastics raised the status of spectacle frames from a dowdy necessity to a fashion accessory. Traditional wire rims dictated a fairly severe and limited style; but the molding potential of plastics offered designers the opportunity to increase the mass and hence the form of the frame without substantially

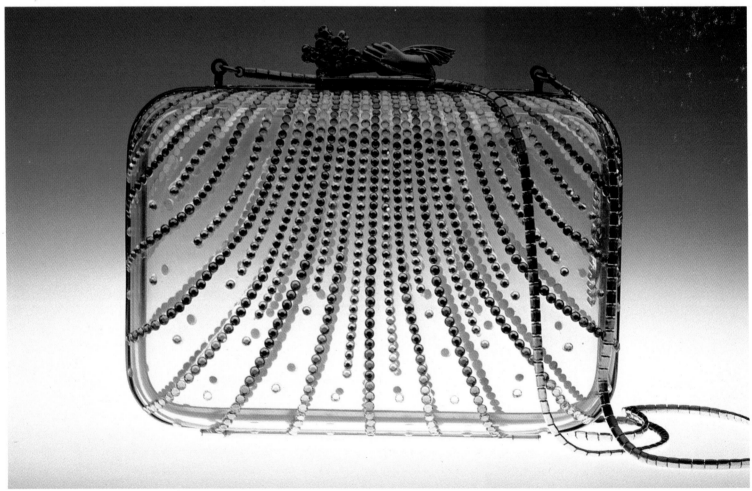

increasing the weight. Also, plastic was more comfortable to wear because, unlike metal, it did not cut into the skin. Round-rimmed "Harold Lloyd" glasses were produced in Celluloid as early as 1918, as were the hand-held glasses called lorgnettes, and well into the twenties. But it was not until the late thirties that "glamorous" sunglasses began to find wide acceptance. Chanel was one of the first (maybe *the* first) designers to don oversized sunglasses; but when privacy-seeking movie stars like Garbo appeared in public wearing sunglasses, the fashion was launched wholesale. Cellulose acetate, still the most commonly used plastic for eyeglass frames, was first used for this purpose in the mid-thirties because it could be injection-molded and therefore mass produced. (Celluloid could not be injection-molded.) Injection-molding accommodated any style, from the fairly sedate, heavy round rims to outlandish Pop creations of the sixties in which frames might be shaped like musical notes, or spell the word "ZOOM" or flare into butterfly wings studded with rhinestones. Such novelty frames are a collecting specialty among those with an interest in kitsch or Pop Art; but plastic collectors often prefer simpler frames in which the material itself is shown to advantage.

Clothing

Plastic materials take many forms in the fashion industry, not the least of which are as textiles woven from synthetic fibers. The synthetic textile industry is not considered part of the plastics industry because its product is so far removed in function and appearance

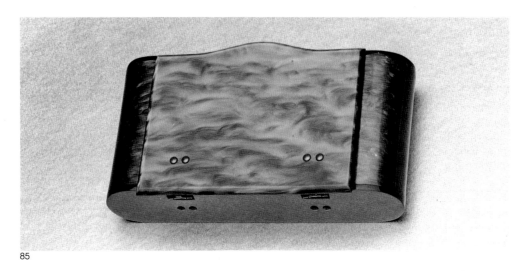

85

from molded products; but in fact the basic materials are the same. Rayon, the first man-made fiber, was originally spun from pure cellulose; nylon and polyester from petrochemical derivatives. When produced in sheet or film form, these, and other, plastics abound as trimming materials for dresses and millinery. It is interesting to realize that the delicate iridescent sequins found on dresses from the twenties are basically of the same material—cellulose acetate—as the slinky rayon acetate dress produced in great quantity in the thirties. Outside of museums with vast representative collections of clothing, few private collectors express interest in synthetics. Often, however, they do not realize that items of rayon clothing—notably the "Joan Crawford" dresses with their architectural shoulders and often tiered pleating—are at least semi-synthetics, as are many of the brightly printed Hawaiian shirts from the fifties.

Elsa Schiaparelli introduced synthetics to couture primarily as rayon crepe;

but she is reported to have made pink "glass" dresses from a material called Rhodophane that was probably cellophane. This was not surprising given her penchant for surrealistic fashions that produced, among other things, hats shaped like inverted high heels and lamp chops. Schiaparelli also decorated her famous snug-fitting evening jackets with all sorts of non-traditional trimmings that sometimes included plastic fruits, flowers, and buttons (page 65). In this sense Schiaparelli was way ahead of the young designers of the sixties who used plastics to create extreme space-age clothing that was often unwearable but ingenious and amusing from the point of view of pure costume. The most memorable designer was the iconoclastic young Spaniard Paco Rabanne, whose subliminal inspiration may well have been the sequin. Rabanne took the sequin and made it larger and sturdier until it became not simply a trimming but a component itself. Each dime-sized plas-

86. Spectacle frames marked only "Made in Italy" were discovered in a long-established optometrist shop going out of business. They date from the 1940s when oversized frames were beginning to enjoy wide popularity. *Douglas Taylor*

87. Sensual wraparound sunglasses were designed in the late 1960s by Bernard Kayman. The one-piece form was produced with injection-molded cellulose acetate. *Photo: Ferdinand Boesch, from "Plastic as Plastic," the American Craft Museum of the American Craft Council, 1968–69; Bonniers*

88. A silk glove ornamented with plastic domes was designed in the 1930s by Elsa Schiaparelli. *Photo: Brooklyn Museum, gift of Paula Peralto Ramos and Arturo Ramos*

86

87

tic disc was perforated so that it could be joined with metal rings to others to construct "no-sew" chainmail dresses. Rabanne's designs sold at Lord & Taylor's Fantasia boutique in 1966 for about $300.00 ($100.00 for a tank top) and were intended to be worn over white body stockings. A year later Mass Originals sold a do-it-yourself kit for only $15.00 that provided all the necessary parts plus a pair of pliers for assembly. Rabanne was featured in the "Fabulous Fashions 1907-1967" exhibit at the Metropolitan Museum's Costume Institute. The catalog explained that Rabanne had started as an architecture student then turned to plastic accessories and then to clothing design. He opened his own house in Paris in 1966. His disc dresses were called "stark" and "futuristic" and his methods of molding and welding "remarkable and new." Rabanne carried his linked disc idea to patched fur and leather dresses and coats and ultimately to masses of buttons laced together with wire. Georgina Howell, author of *In Vogue*, wrote that in 1966 everyone was "talking about Paco Rabanne and his plastic fashion sculpture. Nearly all designers are infected with the mirage of 'space age fashion.'"

Among the designers similarly infected was Diana Dew, who created a black vinyl minidress for Paraphernalia with 18 plastic windows that could light up when the hip-worn battery pack was activated. Betsey Johnson offered a see-through blue vinyl strapless mini (thoughtfully provided with soft nylon bust pads). Plastic even tempted notables from the conservative ranks such as Oscar de la Renta, who created an

evening raincoat of clear vinyl studded with enormous faceted rhinestones. The effect was of great glistening drops of water, actually quite beautiful when contemplated on the hanger but a steamy experience on bare shoulders. In France, the venerable Dior and flamboyant Chloé used plastics accordingly suited to their images.

The dry-cleaning establishment was not amused, however, by such go-go fashions. In 1966, the *Bulletin of the National Institute of Dry Cleaning* expressed the exasperation that many women and manufacturers probably shared: "You may feel that today's fashions are 'unsafe at any speed.' We are in the era of the fashion gimmick. And we will need to live with it until fashion changes and becomes 'rational' again."

Vanity Items

Collectors who buy Celluloid vanity sets produced in the first decades of this century often share the attitude of the original owners who sought inexpensive simulations of more luxurious sets. Imitations of ivory, mother-of-pearl, and tortoiseshell were, and are, ten times cheaper than the real thing. Today, individual items are still cheap, but complete sets in good condition are extremely rare and can be costly.

Between about 1900 and 1920, Celluloid manufacturers produced vanity sets by the hundreds of thousands. They normally were fitted out with at least ten pieces, including comb and brush, one or more hand mirrors, a powder box, a hair receiver (a box with a hole in the lid through which hair from the brush could be stuffed), small containers for pins and ointments, cylin-

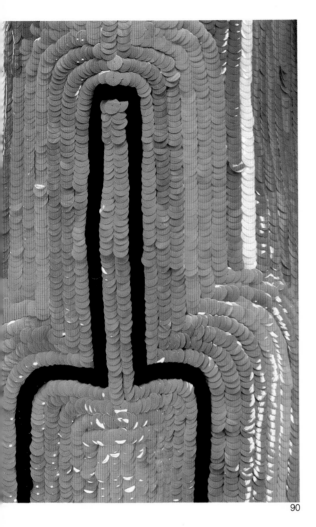

90

89–90. Dresses by the fashion designers Paco Rabanne, left, Dior, center, and Chloé all date from the 1960s, the decade when even the haute couture was using plastic to achieve futuristic and modernistic effects. Rabanne's fetching chainmail mini was created by joining hundreds of plastic discs with tiny metal rings. Dior's velvet cocktail dress has a hem thickly appliqued with vinyl "flowers." Chloé's Art Deco revival sheath is entirely covered in hand-appliqued, nickel-sized plastic sequins (detail above). *Metropolitan Museum of Art, gift of Mr. Paco Rabanne, 1967; gift of Mrs. Charles Wrightsman, 1970; and gift of Mrs. Robert A. Fowler, 1978*

drical containers for cotton, a tray, manicuring implements including scissors and nail buffer, an atomizer, and sometimes a glove stretcher, button hook, and even picture frames. All of these items were thin-walled and thus suitable for blow-molding or thermoforming, the usual means of Celluloid fabrication.

Many collectors consider the most elegant of the pre-1920 sets to be the creamy-colored "French Ivory" or "Ivory Pyralin" ensembles that were produced by Du Pont or companies using their materials. Sets marked "French Ivory" were in fact made in France and exported. Occasionally such "Ivory" sets are found with engraved monograms as was commonly done with real ivory. Leather traveling cases often were fitted with ivory-like Celluloid implements and toilet articles; and because the case has protected them over the years, they often are found in better condition than the dressing table accessories.

The earliest sets usually are styled after antique reproductions; but during the twenties and thirties sets were produced in stunning Art Deco designs characterized by abstract motifs in vivid contrasting colors such as black and chartreuse, black and orange, and such. Multicolored effects were achieved by handpainting or by inlaying one color plastic into another. Additional decorative effects often were achieved with rhinestones and touches of metal trim.

Designers of vanity sets are largely unknown, with a few notable exceptions. In the early thirties the renowned jewelry and glass designer René Lalique created the cherry-embossed powder box on page 82 that may have

been part of a larger set. Since Lalique is known to have used Celluloid to create engraved invitations to his showings, it is probable that he used the same material for the boxes. About the same time, the noted interior designer Paul T. Frankl created two striking Art Deco plastic sets, probably for the American Celluloid Company. They are pictured in his book *Form and ReForm* but their production history is unknown.

The Celluloid vanity items found today often exhibit irreparable damage such as burns, or staining from contact with alcohol, or warping from having been left in the sun or near direct heat. Acrylic sets, which generally date from the forties and fifties, often exhibit the same type of damage since, like Celluloid, acrylic is a thermoplastic and subject to many of the same ravages. With very few exceptions, such as the silver-ornamented mirror on page 81, acrylic sets from that era tend to be of the gaudy dime-store variety. By the fifties, industrial designers such as Raymond Loewy had begun to streamline and otherwise modernize vanity items, which by then extended little beyond a mirror, comb, and brush set.

The vogue for the elaborate, formal vanity set—and the use of Celluloid— began to wane as commercial cosmetic packaging became more elaborate and cosmetics in general became more diversified and specialized. Women found that elegantly packaged powders, creams, and lotions that could be proudly displayed, then disposed of and replaced, made an assortment of generic containers obsolete. The American industrial designer John Vassos takes credit for introducing, in

91

91. Ivory Celluloid accessories for a baby's dresser include a four-inch picture frame and a hand-painted cotton-wool dispenser. Both date from about 1920. *Dean Carpaccio; Walton Rawls*

92. A setting for antique Celluloid vanity items evokes the period just before 1920. Plastics include a French atomizer, an octagonal hair receiver filled with potpourri, a hand mirror marked "Ivory Py-ra-lin" (a Du Pont product), and a nail buffer marked "Amerith." The ornate box at left is a turn-of-the-century container for Celluloid collars and cuffs, as the embossing indicates. It is coated with a thin film of Celluloid and decorated in gold paint. *Author's collection; collar box, Irving Barbershop Antiques*

92

93

94

1924, the first plastic screw cap on a cosmetic bottle. As quoted by John Pulos in *American Design Ethic*, Vassos reported that his innovation increased sales by 700 percent, and added that his cosmetic bottles often were recycled during Prohibition as gin flasks. But plastic caps or jar lids were still considered a novelty in the mid-thirties, with the plain cylindrical or ball-shape being most common. Phenolic plastics were invariably used when the contents of the bottle contained an organic solvent such as alcohol, while cellulose acetate and acrylics came into use for powder and rouge containers. Examples of early cosmetic packaging are rarer than the vanity items precisely because the former were intended as disposables.

In the mid-thirties some plastic molders produced decorative boxes for use as product packaging that could be reused as containers for vanity items or jewelry or cigarettes and odds and ends. The red and black box on page 30, which imitates Oriental lacquerware and is among the most successful Art Deco plastic designs, actually was produced in an industrial grade plastic that ordinarily would have been used as electrical insulation.

As women began to enter the work force in greater numbers it became necessary to transform vanity items into portable forms that could easily fit into the handbag. A comb or brush, a compact, a refillable lipstick case, and a scent bottle had, of course, been standard traveling equipment for modern women since the twenties; but plastics lightened the load considerably. The dichotomy between luxury materials

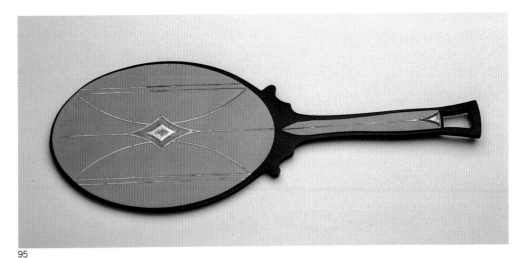

95

96

and plastics persisted with precious or plated metals occupying the upper echelons and plastics doing their best to provide affordable glamor. Acrylic was unquestionably the most glamorous plastic for this purpose because of its transparency.

Cosmetic Packaging

Cosmetic preparations packaged in all-plastic containers were unusual until the late forties and early fifties when acid-

93. Vanity items dating from about 1910 include, left, a gentleman's stud box of Celluloid; center, a molded shellac hand mirror painted white; and a tiny Celluloid ointment container. *J. Harry DuBois*

94. A powder bowl of pearlized green Celluloid has a removable amber liner. Its design with three ball feet is in the English style of the early 1920s. The blush-pink down puff is French and, with a long translucent handle, rare. *Douglas Taylor*

95. This Art Deco hand mirror from the 1920s is made of Celluloid. *Jacaranda*

96. A c.1940 hand mirror with beveled acrylic handle and sterling silver ornament is unmarked. Part of a set, including mirror-backed hairbrush and comb, it is probably of European origin. *Dom La Raia*

resistant thermoplastics such as polystyrene became available for low-cost high-volume injection molding. Because thermoplastics were also light in weight and infinitely colorful, they were enthusiastically adopted by the large cosmetic firms such as Max Factor and Avon; but even more exclusive companies such as Dunhill, who produced toiletries for men, and Erno Laszlo, a pioneer of the scientific approach to skin care, did not hesitate to experiment with molded design for an elite clientele. In 1954, Carl Otto created award-winning packaging designs for Laszlo that eschewed cloying five-and-dime pastels for neutral colors and classical forms in simulated marble that suggested the richness of the product. Elsa Perretti's organically sculptural plastic scent bottle designed for Halston in the seventies conveys a similar message: that the material need not be precious to express elegance.

FACING PAGE:
97. René Lalique created this three-inch-square powder box in the 1930s. Signed along the topmost cherry stem, it probably was made of thermoformed Celluloid. Examples have been found in black as well as red, but all are rare. *50:Fifty*

98. The confettilike pattern of this four-inch-long vanity box probably was created by compressing bits of multicolored Celluloid stock into a thin sheet that was then thermoformed in a mold. *Richard Utilla*

99. Hand-painted, tiny, plastic solid-scent boxes date from the 1920s. Labeled "Bag Dabs, France, Edouardo," each contains a still-fragrant scent, one of chypre, the other of lilac. *Fred Silberman*

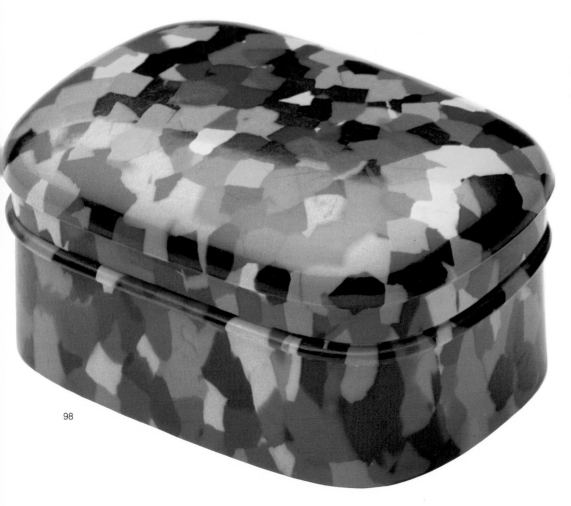

98

99

100

101

100. The body of this vanity jar is simply a section sliced from a cylinder of cast phenolic resin. The lid and base were cut to fit from sheet, and the whole thing was polished to a high gloss. *Carol Ferranti*

101. This powder box, marked "a la Corbeille Royale," is molded of an industrial grade phenolic resin and was found in a Brussels flea market. *Author's collection*

102

103

104

102. The lid of this Celluloid box simulates a pinwheel of goldstone and marble. *Richard Utilla*

103. Celluloid vanity boxes for pins, left, and powder may be of European origin. The powder box, in particular, which is shaped like a shield and bears a heraldic pattern known as an engrailed line, may well be British. *Richard Utilla*

104. A cube-topped box, 4½ inches high, is made of marbleized green phenolic resin. *Douglas Taylor*

FACING PAGE:
105. An acrylic compact designed in 1946 by the toiletry manufacturer Roger and Gallet measures four inches square. The sunburst medallion was molded separately and hand-applied and the face was hand-painted. It was manufactured in America by Donmak Creations Co. *Susan Ellsworth*

106

107

108

Specialized Grooming Equipment

Toothbrushes were among the first toilet articles made of plastic. Early examples with natural bristles appear to be molded of Celluloid or casein plastics and frequently have their own cylindrical containers for travel purposes. Shaving brushes acquired colorful cast phenolic resin handles in the early thirties, about the time that molded phenolics and urea plastics were coming into use

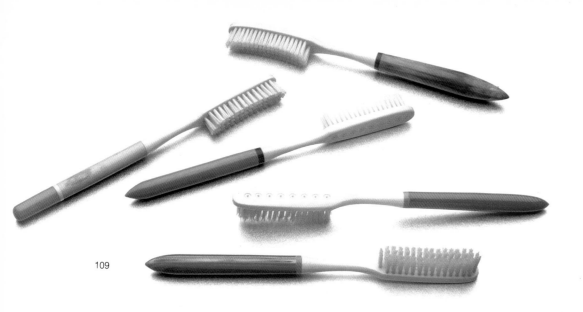

109

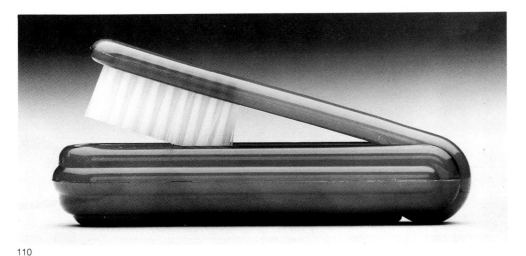

110

106. A molded-glass shaving lotion bottle is capped with a cubistic plastic head. *Primavera Gallery*

107. A multicolored Celluloid cigarette case appears to be painted with an abstract landscape. *Richard Utilla*

108. Shaving brushes made of cast phenolic resin date from 1940, when the manufacturer advertised them as "Brushes by Rubberset . . . Beauty by Catalin." *Douglas Taylor*

109. French toothbrushes from the 1920s were made of either Celluloid or casein plastic. In the brush at top, an attempt was made to create a millefiori effect, something ordinarily achievable only in glass. *Douglas Taylor*

110. A folding toothbrush from Denmark was designed in 1982 by Buch-Deichmann. *Author's collection*

for small electrical grooming equipment.

The electrification of all types of appliances, including grooming devices, started early in the century when small fractional horsepower motors were first developed. Before 1920, motor housings for implements like vibrators (supposedly the first electric personal care product) and hair dryers were all metal, very heavy, and prone to heating up. This situation improved with the intro-

duction of plastics, which were not only lighter but good heat insulators. The first electric shaver in America was introduced by Schick in 1931. It had a black phenolic housing and at $25.00 sold three thousand units that year. By 1936, a million were on the market at sharply reduced prices, along with many competing brands such as Remington and Sunbeam. In 1948, Norelco introduced a streamlined razor with an

innovative rotary action shaving head. The design, manufactured in America by North American Philips, was an improvement on similar European models that GIs brought back after the war. While subsequent models became increasingly compact and more comfortable to handle, the original design remains one of the latest and most dramatic examples of small-scale streamlining in America.

2 NECESSITIES

FACING PAGE:
111. A European-made Bakelite coffee grinder from the 1930s, marked "PeDe," is the star attraction in this collection of vintage plastic kitchen equipment. Other pieces include the Swiss tin canister with Bakelite lid marked "Hermit S.A.-Berne-Suisse" and the chrome and plastic egg timer. The melamine Texasware cups and saucers are from the 1950s. Future plastic collectibles include the bear-shaped honey dispenser and Domino sugar shaker. *Grinder, Maison Gerard; canister and Texasware, author's collection; timer and flatware, Kenneth Kneitel*

OVERLEAF:
112. Kenneth Kneitel's collection of plastic-handled kitchen utensils and flatware dates from the 1930s and '40s. The majority are red, green, and amber, the most popular plastic colors for housewares of the period. Although few are marked with a manufacturer's name, handle shapes can sometimes identify a particular maker. The ribbed, tapered handles, for example, were made by Androck. Utensils include spoons, spatulas, sieves, pastry cutters, a pie crimper, cheese and butter cutters, bottle openers, scrapers, a barbeque set, and assorted serving pieces. Salt and pepper shakers are Lustroware from 1949; contemporary "spatterware" melamine mixing bowl is Boonton Molding. The gram measure is Danish.

Kitchen Equipment

There was probably no other room in the home but the kitchen where concepts of functionalism and modernism found such quick and eager acceptance in the 1920s and '30s. It was logical that in an area where utility, rather than "decor," had always been the foremost consideration, ideas that purported to save time and energy had no trouble taking hold. Also, industrial materials such as iron, tin, and brass always had been essential to the execution of kitchen tasks. So there was little ingrained prejudice to overcome against new materials such as plastic and stainless steel. Both brought functional and in many cases esthetic improvements to kitchen equipment.

Tremendous changes in the design of kitchens began after World War I with the gradual disappearance of the "servant class," those who always had lived-in and who had been the fairly exclusive inhabitants of drab utilitarian kitchens. The kitchen, as in the 18th century, became more and more a multi-use room inhabited by housewives for long hours and by families for whom it was often a dining room as well. Designers therefore urged both the adoption of labor-saving devices and the transformation of the room by light and color into a place that was not only efficient but bright and cheerful too. The redesign of kitchen equipment was a monumental task undertaken with great seriousness by manufacturers together with industrial designers of the thirties. Their efforts were reinforced by the art and design community, which in the late 1920s had begun to take up the cause of the everyday object and machine art in general. In the late thirties, for example, the Museum of Modern Art had begun a series of exhibitions of *Useful Household Objects Under $5* that included kitchen and tableware as well as objects for personal use chosen for their good design.

Plastics were adopted both to brighten and to streamline utensils and appliances. The jewel-like colors of cast phenolic resin suddenly began to appear as handles and knobs for stainless steel utensils, flatware, and chrome-

Federal Modern

This 1943 photograph illustrated an article in the Springfield (Mass.) *Sunday Republican* about Federally funded housing for defense workers. The Lucy Mallory Villages, as they were called, were designed by Royal Barry Mills, known locally as an architect of Colonial-style housing. The homes featured a modest yet modernized kitchen equipped with new chrome and plastic appliances, including a portable radio, electric toaster, and waffle iron. Mrs. Carl E. Farnham, who posed for the photo, recalled that the "modern" appliances did not always live up to manufacturers' promises. The waffle iron, she says, always stuck. *Photo: Mrs. Carl E. Farnham*

113

114

116

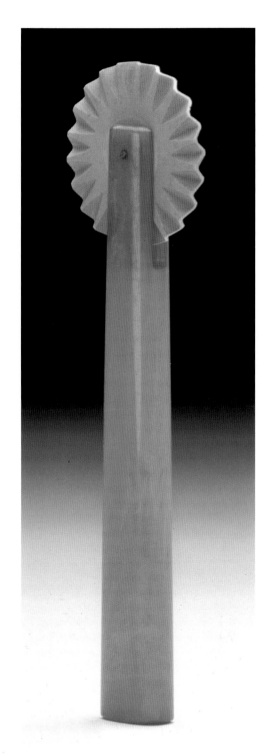

115

113–114. Bakelite thermoses (above) and an assortment of kitchen equipment from France and England are popular with European collectors. The group below includes a covered cake dish, far right, reamers, a food storage box, syrup dispenser, and bowl. *Photos: Galerie Roudillon; Christian Gervais*

115. A pie crimper from the 1930s is made of cast phenolic resin. *Linda Campbell Franklin*

116. This scouring brush was designed in 1975 by Ahlstrom & Ehrich Design AB, a Swedish firm, for the Norwegian Jordan Company. Heller Designs, Inc., imported it into the United States in 1978. *Photo: Heller Design*

117

117. The phenolic sewing box with a removable spool tray was made in the 1930s by the Domart Company of Glenside, Pa. *Linda Campbell Franklin*

118. This electric "hot water bottle" is actually a rigid phenolic molding made in England in the 1930s as a bed warmer. *Galerie Metropol; photo: Osterkorn*

119. The A. C. Gilbert Kitchen Kit, redesigned in 1939 by Robert Heller, was the first mixer to have an all-plastic housing. The new design was credited with increasing sales by more than 30 percent. *Reprinted from* Durez Plastics News, *June, 1939.*

120. The small desk fan with an all-phenolic housing has replaceable safety blades of grosgrain ribbon. Manufactured for Sears by Diehl, the electrical division of Singer, it sold as both the Diehl Ribbonaire and the Airflow Safan from the 1930s to the 1950s. *Maison Gerard*

118

ware—tea and coffee sets, and cocktail shakers, for example. This was the same plastic that adorned many a Depression-era housewife in the form of jewelry and buttons. And, in fact, in 1936 one manufacturer—A&J Kitchen Tool Company—promoted their "Ritz" line of plastic-handled utensils as "kitchen jewelry." Brilliant reds and greens were the most common colors, as they had been for the painted wooden-handled ware of the 1920s. (No one knows who had determined these to be the housewife's favorite colors. The idea persisted for decades.) Sometimes contrasting colors were combined to create stripes, chevrons, or even, in very rare cases, polka dots. Patriotic red, white, and blue striped handles were produced during the war. In some cases, plastic was used to form the entire utensil—common after World War II but rare in the 1930s. The brightly colored plastic pie crimper on page 93 would have been a true novelty in a kitchen accustomed to wooden-

121

handled tinware and wireware.

Plastics were promoted for their beauty, but also because they were more hygienic than wood. They were nonporous and, therefore, did not harbor bacteria; and the entire implement could be boiled and sterilized if necessary. Plastics also allowed the implement shank to be imbedded permanently in the handle without chance of loosening over the years, as often happened with wood. Plastics also eliminated the chronically chipping paint on wooden handles. In combination with stainless steel, plastic could be promoted as both germproof and rustproof, two strong selling points in an efficiency-conscious era.

American manufacturers were less apt than Europeans to use the dark, industrial, molded phenolic resin—Bakelite—for objects that came into direct contact with food. But during the thirties in Europe it was common to find such things as reamers, egg cups, coffee grinders, cutlery handles, and serving bowls in handsome mottled Bakelite. European manufacturers tried consciously to imitate wood and ceramic materials with Bakelite; but, as in America, no one was ever fooled and the material was viewed as an inexpensive novelty—which it was—yet practical and serviceable.

In America, molded phenolic resin, an efficient heat insulator, was used almost exclusively for the redesign of electrical appliances and for cookware handles. The most familiar examples of such moldings are motor housings, handles for irons, toasters, and fancy glass percolators, and for washing machine impellers. (Outside of the kitchen

122

123

124

125

121. Gino Colombini's polyethylene dustpan was introduced by Kartell in 1958 and produced until 1984. *Kartell*

122. The Hoover vacuum cleaner, Model 150, redesigned by Henry Dreyfuss in 1936, was the first to utilize a molded plastic motor housing. The streamlined design in "battleship gray" and "stratosphere blue" was appealing, but the fact that the use of plastics decreased the cleaner's weight was credited with increasing sales. *Photo: Hoover Company Historical Center*

123. A cartoon published in *Durez Plastics News* in 1940 dramatized the benefit of decreasing the weight of appliances through the use of plastic moldings. *Reprinted from* Durez Plastics News, *May, 1940.*

124. One of the most spectacular electric iron designs was the 1946 Petipoint with its streamlined metal fins devised as a cooling system for the sturdy molded handle. *Reprinted from* Durez Plastics News, *May, 1940.*

125. A French steam iron by Novex has an integral handle and housing of maroon Bakelite. *Photo: Galerie Roudillon; Christian Gervais*

126. This polystyrene watering pitcher was designed and manufactured by the noted Swedish firm of Gustavesberg Fabriker AB in the late 1960s. Twelve inches high and five inches in diameter at the base, it provides—apart from a striking sculptural form—a narrow neck that is easy to grip. *Photo: Swedish Information Service*

127. Neal Small, an American artist and designer, created these pitchers in the 1970s by sculpting mouths into acrylic cylinders. *Photo: Neal Small*

126

phenolic resin was used for desk and office equipment, lighting, radio, television, and phonograph cases, as discussed below.) In most instances the inner works of the appliance remained unchanged while the designer supplied a sleek new, often streamlined sheathing for it. In his textbook *Industrial Design*, published in 1940, Harold Van Doren used redesigns by two leading industrial designers as object lessons in how plastics and styling can result in dramatic sales increases.

In the first case, Van Doren cited Robert Heller's redesign of the A. C. Gilbert Kitchen Kit, a venerable all-purpose metal workhorse that was mechanically efficient but ugly and cumbersome to handle. Heller created a streamlined plastic housing that reduced the overall weight of the appliance by 32 percent. Van Doren wrote that although the price remained about the same ($26.75 to $29.95), sales rose by nearly a third in the first year. Unquestionably, Heller's design also contributed considerably to the mixer's sales success. According to Durez, supplier of the molding resin, the redesign was most interesting from the standpoint of product engineering. "Notes on Product Improvement" published in the *Durez News* in 1938 explained that "each molding is accurate to a few thousandths of an inch. Drive shaft bearing surfaces, drive shaft guides,

interlocking sections, assembly pin holes, speed selector markings—all these are molded into the various parts in one operation." Heller's was a historic first use of plastic for a mixer as was Henry Dreyfuss's use of it for the redesign of the Hoover Model 150 vacuum cleaner in 1935. Like Heller, Dreyfuss created a streamlined housing combined with the new lightweight metal magnesium that reduced the weight of the appliance by 30 percent. Since the earlier vacuum cleaners had been extremely heavy cast-steel contraptions, the weight factor was in this case even more significant for the women who had to push them around each day; and, according to Van Doren, again sales boomed. By 1939, the Hoover had lost several more pounds as the number of plastic parts increased to twenty.

One of the foremost promoters of plastic housewares was John R. Morgan, merchandise designer for the Sears, Roebuck Company from the mid- to late-thirties. Morgan had designed the first plastic radio to be carried by Sears (page 138) and believed "the use of plastics is particularly adaptable to many articles for retail distribution because of their diversity in color and color combinations. They adapt themselves," he continued in a 1937 *Modern Plastics* article, "to all manner of forms that were impossible in other types of manufacturing and made possible unique effects because of their flexibility." One of the most striking designs introduced by Morgan was the Airflow Safan (page 95) molded entirely of Bakelite and in production from 1935 to 1950 (or later) when it sold for $12.95.

128. Although embossed with typical streamlined motifs, these polystyrene beverage pitchers manage to look like plump comic characters. They were manufactured in the 1940s by the Burroughs Company of Los Angeles. *Susan Ellsworth*

129. These molded polyethylene ketchup containers were the first squeeze-bottle food dispensers. Designed by Morris Friedman, they were mass-produced in the 1950s for home use and then adopted widely by restaurants. These three show how the mold developed from the realistic small model (marked "Squeezit Corp.") to a much simplified squarish version at center. *J. Harry DuBois*

128   129

130

131

130. A canister set molded by Columbus Plastic Products in 1949 was standard equipment in many postwar American kitchens. *Photo: National Housewares Manufacturers Association; from* The Housewares Story

131. When these Tupperware food-storage bowls of flexible polyethylene were introduced in the late 1940s, *House Beautiful* magazine called them "fine art for $.39." *Photo: Tupperware*

132. These bowls made in England in the late 1920s or '30s are typical "Beatl" ware, a then-new urea-formaldehyde plastic. For kitchen and tableware use, urea was an improvement over Bakelite in that it made light colors possible in thermosetting plastic for the first time. By the 1950s, urea had been replaced by melamine in tableware. *Richard Utilla*

Morgan also appreciated the high polish and scratch-resistant finishes of molded plastics and, of course, their price—considering that since the 19th century Sears catalogs carried the tag "cheapest supply house on earth." Sears and other mail-order houses most surely appreciated the savings in postage earned by plastics because of their reduced weight in shipping, a factor still of prime consideration.

The substantial look and feel of phenolics, and the fact that despite years of use they retain much of their high gloss and bright color accounts for their popularity with collectors. The newer plastics that came into use during and after World War II for storage containers and dinnerware, and that were subject to constant wear and tear, have survived less well. Still, out of the ocean of plasticware that began to swamp consumers in the fifties emerged two household words that deserve mention—

Tupperware and Melmac. Both are trade names that have come to stand for the generic categories of plastic food storage ware and melamine dinnerware. Collectors have only begun to explore these areas and the more recent products from the 1960s and '70s.

In 1945 Earl S. Tupper, a chemist from Farnumsville, Massachusetts, began producing his injection-molded polyethylene tumblers and food storage containers in delicate frosted pastels.

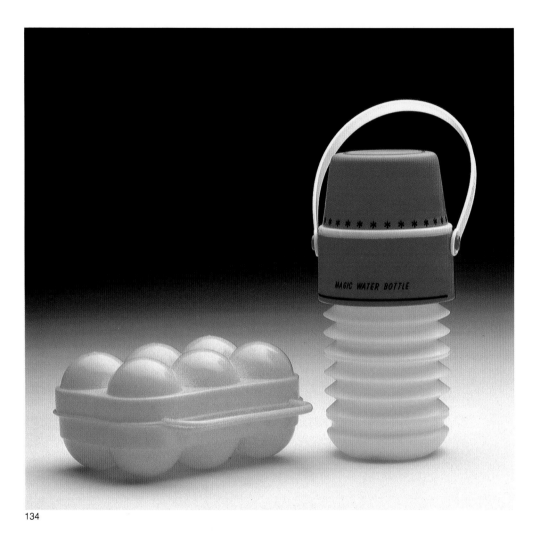

134

133. An English picnic hamper dating from the late 1920s or early '30s is fitted out with service for four in "Bandalasta" ware, a urea-formaldehyde plastic. The set contains plates, teacups and saucers, nesting tumblers, seven food containers, three thermoses, and one bottle, presumably for spirits. The forks are marked "Sheffield Plate & Cutlery Co. Ltd. Made in England, Coracle NS [Nickel Silver]." The knives are marked "G. W. Scott & Sons Ltd. England," indicating that the set was assembled from various sources by the manufacturer, Coracle, whose label is affixed to the inside of the lid. Purchased in a New York City antique shop, it is a rare find with no missing pieces. *Ned Foss*

134. Camper's equipment includes an egg carrier made in France and an expandable "Magic Water Bottle" made in Japan. *Author's collection*

In 1947, *House Beautiful* magazine called his wares "fine art for 39 cents," and Tupper lost no time parlaying that endorsement into an empire. The original line of about a dozen items has expanded to more than 200, including not only food and storage containers but also toys and horticultural products sold in more than 30 foreign countries. (Tupper supplies special "exotic" items for special needs, such as a Seaweed Keeper in Japan and a Tortilla Keeper in Mexico.) Tupper originally sold his ware through the usual retail outlets, but when he developed the now famous "Tupperware seal"—requiring that the lid be flexed and the air "burped" out to render it airtight—he realized that it needed to be demonstrated in order to be fully appreciated. To this end Tupper invented the home party system in 1951, the method by which all Tupperware is now sold. Tupper was an innovator on many levels: in the use of polyethylene and in his marketing techniques that pioneered the recruitment of consumers as a grass roots sales force.

Plastic Dinnerware

Molded plastic dinnerware was truly a phenomenon of the fifties, particularly as concerns the designs of Russel Wright. But actually it had been around since the late 1920s. The urea–formaldehyde plastic known familiarly in England as Beetleware, where it had been

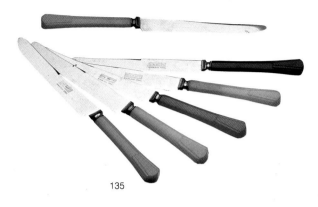

135

136

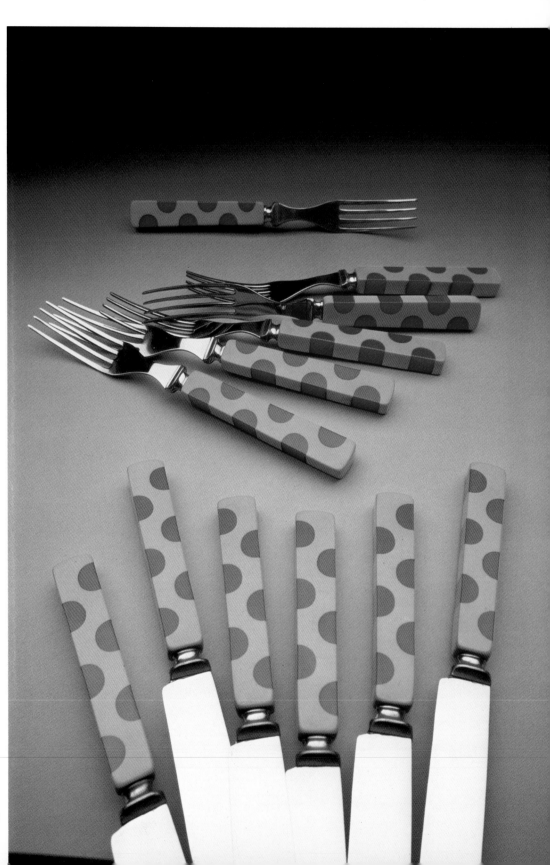

135–137. Plastic-handled flatware brightened up many a Depression-era table, but none so well as the polka-dot set, right. The translucent red dots are inlaid in the opaque yellow plastic to form chunky ½ inch-thick handles attached to Cardinal stainless steel. Never used, the set is a mint-condition rarity. The pastels and black chevron design, above, demonstrate the range of styles available, from pretty to sophisticated. *Kenneth Kneitel (polka dots; pastels); Richard Utilla (black)*

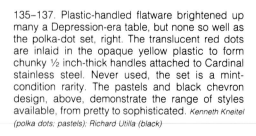

137

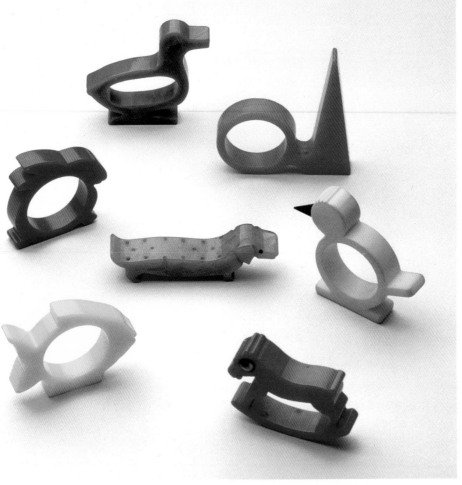

138

139

138. Napkin rings in mostly animal forms surround a dachshund toothpick holder. All are carved from cast phenolic resin and date from the late 1930s and '40s. The rocking horse with green eyes is rare; the chicken is more common and currently being reproduced. The Trylon and Perisphere, upper right, commemorates the 1939 World's Fair. *Douglas Taylor*

139. Diamond-shaped corncob holders of cast phenolic resin date from the 1940s, about the time when backyard barbeques became popular. *Susan Ellsworth*

140. Franklin D. Roosevelt's dog Fala, a Scottie, prompted a raft of novelties in its image, such as this set of napkin rings. Made of cast phenolic resin, they have hand-painted faces. *Susan Ellsworth*

140

141

141. An individual chrome and plastic tea or coffee service made by the Manning-Bowman Co., of Meriden, Conn., bears the company's name and motto—"means best." In typical machine-age style, no attempt is made to disguise the tiny screws by which plastic and metal are joined. *Richard Utilla*

developed, was used extensively to produce dinnerplates, bowls, and picnic sets in light and mottled colors. English manufacturers include Brookes and Adams Ltd. (who produced "Bandalasta ware"), Streetly, GEC, Witton, and DeLaRue. American Cyanamid brought the formula to the United States, where it was also known as Beetleware. Although urea was a strong thermosetting plastic, it did not survive well in situations where it was constantly being immersed in water. It tended to crack and fade because the natural fillers, usually wood pulp or cotton, had poor moisture resistance. The pieces that survive in good condition and have retained their distinctive colors, such as the bowls on page 103, most certainly escaped heavy use.

In design, urea dinnerware invariably reproduced traditional forms of china such as footed bowls and flanged plates, which it was meant to replace,

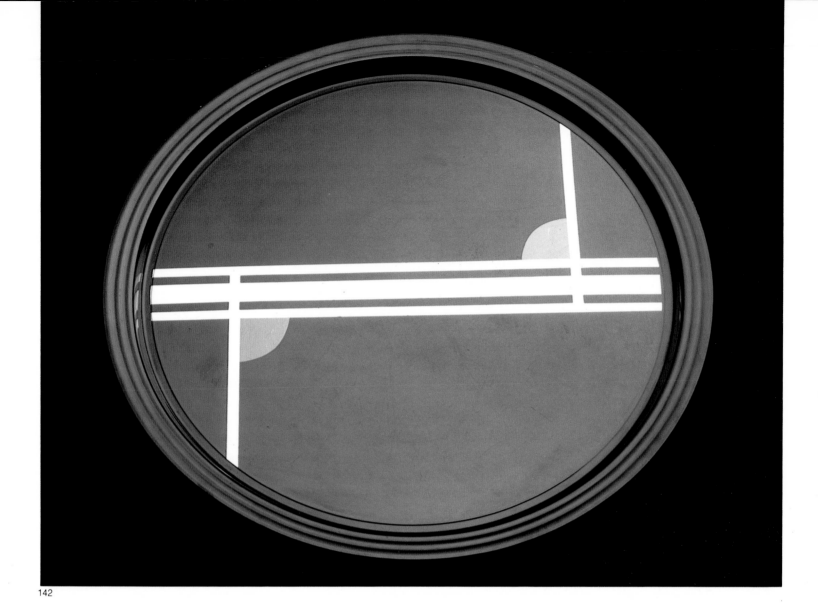

142

at least for everyday use. In the U.S. it was also adopted for the manufacture of radio premiums in the 1930s, the most famous of which are the Little Orphan Annie Shake-up Mug offered by the makers of Ovaltine and the Skippy Bowl promoted by Wheaties.

Promoters of plastic dinnerware stressed its unbreakability, color, lightness, and cheapness, features that suited it well to institutional use. And, in fact, the U.S. military was persuaded to contract with the Boonton Molding Company of New Jersey to produce prototype designs for the Navy. The plastic used was melamine, the thermoset with acid and water resistance superior to that of both the phenolic and urea plastics.

The success of melamine for the Navy encouraged manufacturers like American Cyanamid to produce it for civilian use. And in 1945 the company contracted with the celebrated industrial

142. Thin strips and segments of silver and blue aluminum inlaid on the face of this molded phenolic tray create a subtle Art Deco design. *Richard Utilla*

110

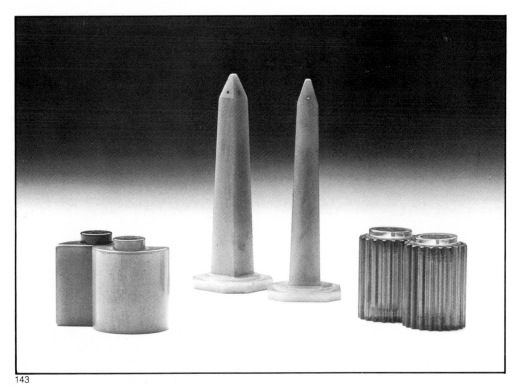

143

143. Sets of small salt and pepper shakers, none over three inches high, were made of cast phenolic resin in the 1930s and '40s. Modules, left, and gearlike design, right, reflect the era's preoccupation with machinery and architecture. The obelisks were souvenirs of the Washington Monument. *Susan Ellsworth; author's collection*

144. A bird with a glowing orange plastic crest and a body carved from a nut adds a touch of whimsy to this unusual salt and pepper set. *Carol Ferranti*

BELOW AND FACING PAGE:
145. "Willie the Penguin," erstwhile mascot of the Kool Cigarette Co. in the 1940s and '50s, was paired with a companion, Millie, to create salt and pepper shaker premiums. *Waves*

144

145

designer Russel Wright to design a line of melamine for them.

Wright's design for Cyanamid was not produced until 1949, under the name Meladur, and then it was used in the Bickford restaurant chain in New York. But in 1953, Wright's "Residential" pattern, created for Northern Industrial Chemical Molding Company of Boston, became the first plasticware to be adopted on a major scale for residential use. Wright's designs were unique,

as were his innovative marketing ideas: he conceived of the "starter set," which permitted consumers to sample the ware without spending much money. As a result "Residential" sold in the millions, not only in department stores but door-to-door as well. The Museum of Modern Art gave it its Good Design award for both 1953 and 1954.

Wright's plasticware was thick-walled and richly colored. Like all melamine, each piece was compression molded

146. Miniature "bombs" are actually polystyrene salt and pepper shakers that were made in the 1940s in bright unwarlike colors. *Susan Ellsworth*

146

147. Early space-age melamine ware from the 1950s, such as the Dallas "Texasware," left, is datable by its muted colors and the presence of cup and saucer—contemporary sets usually feature a mug. *Author's collection*

148. Russel Wright's most successful melamine dinnerware, "Residential," was praised for its organic form and rich colors. Introduced in 1953, it was manufactured by the Northern Industrial Chemical Company and received the Museum of Modern Art's Good Design award for two consecutive years. *Robert Shaw*

149. The "Flair" line of Wright's plastic dinnerware produced in 1959 shows Oriental influence. In this unusual variation called "Ming," Wright imbedded real leaves in the molding. *Robert Shaw*

in a two-part mold that resulted in a seam where the halves meet. But Wright's mold design cleverly placed the seam where it was not apparent. (A visible molding line is the indication of cheaply made ware.)

Wright's success provoked many molders into creating their own lines, and by 1956 there were about 16 firms in the U.S. producing melamine ware. In *The Housewares Story*, Earl Lifshey notes that the molders were often hu-miliated when they attempted to offer plasticware to department store china and glass buyers, who shunted them toward the housewares department; or worse, suggested they sell to institutions and cheap restaurants. As a result, that is where a good deal of the ware is sold today, as well as through discount chains and major supermarket promotions.

Russel Wright's designs were often imitated, particularly the way in which he engineered the cup, allowing the top of the handle to flow into the rim. In 1954, *Industrial Design* magazine surveyed the field of plastic dinnerware and waxed poetic in describing Wright's pieces that "sweep into useful contours without any announcement of beginning and end." Wright's designs were the first to exhibit what has been called organic forms, characterized by sensual sculptural curves. *Industrial Design* judged that the only other plas-

ticware that compared with Wright's esthetically—although it was entirely different stylistically—was the Florence line designed by Irving Harper of George Nelson Associates and produced by the Prolon Division of Prophylactic Brush. Harper based his forms on traditional Japanese lacquerware, an age-old substitute for china, whose simplicity of line and elegance would, he said, "give the material prestige." (In an ironic reversal, the Japanese began to produce melamine "lacquerware" in the early 1980s.) So the choice, said *Industrial Design*, lay between "Wright's amorphism" and the "classic perfection of the Nelson line."

Despite high hopes for acceptance in the home, plastic dinnerware has fought an ongoing battle to survive the competition with low-priced ceramic lines such as Ironstone and Corning's break-resistant ceramic composition Corelle. These products catered to the consumer's ingrained preference for ceramic ware at prices competitive with quality plastics. Plastic producers countered for the most part by continuing to

FACING PAGE:
150. The Florence line of melamine dinnerware designed in the mid-1950s by Irving Harper of George Nelson Associates for Prolon was inspired by Japanese lacquerware. Its graceful lines are atypical of most melamine from the period. *Photo: George Nelson Associates*

151. A red melamine sushi tray made in Japan by Yamato Plastics is a good imitation of natural Oriental lacquerware. It compares favorably in both color and luster with the traditional red lacquer sake cup embellished with the Imperial gold chrysanthemum.
Author's collection; antiques, Walton Rawls

152

153

produce ware that is a plastic imitation of china. Lenox China, for example, introduced a "Golden Harvest" line of melamine in the mid 1950s hoping to interest the upscale audience. Applied decoration in the form of sheaves of wheat would, it was hoped, attract customers with its "traditional elegance"; and even *Industrial Design* magazine heralded the effort, announcing that plastic dinnerware had at last "shaken off its picnic associations and become an element in gracious living." Ultimately, Lenox did not find a receptive market and sold its plastics division in the early 1970s.

In 1972, however, Heller Design introduced Massimo Vignelli's Max I melamine stacking ware in white and a rainbow of vivid colors to the American market. With its space-saving efficiency and high-tech elegance, Vignelli's design represented the first time that melamine had been used in a truly modern sense, that is without stylistic allusions to either organic or traditional ceramic forms. (True, in the 1950s

152–153. Melamine tableware designed by Massimo Vignelli Associates for Heller Design includes, top, the ill-fated Max II cup and saucer, casualty of the unforeseen custom of filling a cup to the brim. In this original version, the open-channeled handle allowed the hot liquid to overflow if filled too high. More successful was the now classic stacking dinnerware, left, with its high-tech edge-wall concept, designed in 1964 for a small company in Milan. Produced in a rainbow of colors by Heller Design since 1969, it received the Compasso d'Oro and is in the design collection of the Museum of Modern Art in New York. *Photos: Vignelli Associates; Mario Carrieri*

Boonton ware had produced an interesting line featuring square plates.) It has had remarkable success in the residential market through careful positioning that avoids discount outlets and associations with knock-offs and flimsy mass-market ware. But most interestingly, the Heller line demonstrated that by allowing plasticware to express its "essence" as an industrial material it could indeed bridge the gap between the patio and the interior, without sacrificing a touch of class.

From a collecting point of view, vintage plastic dinnerware—even the best-selling Russel Wright ware—is today fairly scarce because it was generally tossed out after a few years of steady use. This is understandable because all melamine eventually acquires a scratched surface from cutlery and is regularly demoted to "pet ware." Therefore, finding sets in unused condition, such as the Texasware on page 112, is unusual. Collectors with an eye to the future ought to be stashing away current favorites for posterity.

154. A festive table setting created with an unlikely combination of styles and materials includes high-tech plastic dinnerware on plastic lace with sterling silver flatware. Champagne glasses are crystal, but the deco-revival highball tumblers are acrylic. Place cards are Celluloid silhouettes from about 1910. *Dinnerware, Heller Design; tumblers by Norse Products; stirrers, Kenneth Kneitel; place cards, author's collection; silver and crystal, Walton Rawls*

3 PASTIMES

"First gent: 'Your chess men and pipes do you proud, Robert. I compliment your good taste.'

Second gent: 'A comparatively inexpensive luxury, Walt; they're made of Catalin, the gem of modern industry.'"

Advertisement,
American Catalin Corporation, 1934.

Companies like Catalin that introduced plastic-handled utensils and flatware as "kitchen jewels," easily extended the metaphor to the small objects that pro-

155. The apartment of artist Dennis J. O'Donnell and writer Nick Chergotis is decorated largely with collections of vintage plastic radios, toys, and Depression-era memorabilia, including the National Recovery Act Banner, far right. Interesting examples include the three streamlined Fada radios and the "microphone" on the top shelf, far left. It is actually a radio, distributed as a publicity gimmick in the 1930s or '40s by a Chicago radio station. The tubes are in the top portion, the speaker in the base. It tunes to only one frequency.

vided amusements and diversion for the leisure hours. Cast phenolic resin transformed smoking paraphernalia, games, desk accessories, and more into "onyx," "marble," or "amber" *luxuries* that most people could easily afford. At the same time, the dark, molded phenolics, such as Bakelite, were used for objects subject to constant wear and tear, like camera cases and radio cabinets. Undoubtedly the plastics industry cherished the vision— not far from the truth—of a typical family listening to a plastic radio while members played plastic checkers, smoked with plastic-stemmed pipes, tapped ashes into plastic ashtrays, and jotted notes with a plastic pen at a desk equipped with a handsome Art Deco plastic stationery box. The family's plastic-covered photo album was tucked away in the desk drawer along with the plastic Baby Brownie camera that took the pictures. Even the shiny black telephone was plastic.

If consumers were never really persuaded to think of these things as luxuries, they were impressed with their

156

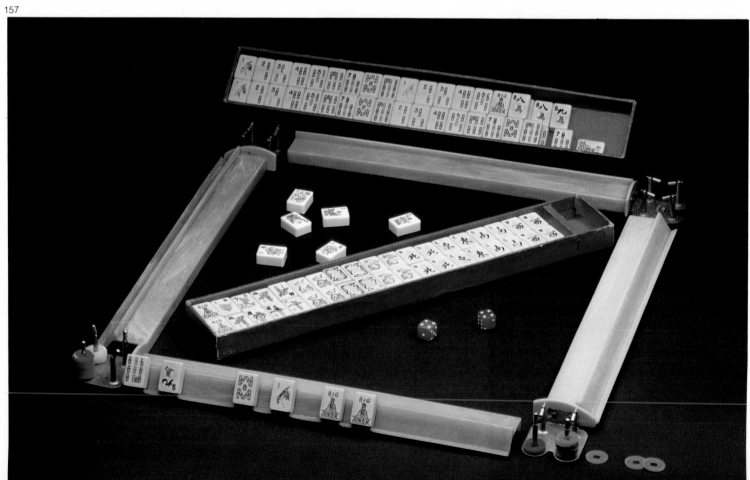

157

156–157. Games and gaming pieces made of cast phenolic resin in the 1930s include, top, poker chips, dominoes, chess pieces, and a word-game dreadle; and, below, the sherbert-colored tile racks for a Mah-Jongg set. *Douglas Taylor; Maison Gerard*

158. A comical palm-sized French ashtray from the 1920s provides a cigarette holder in the form of a molded head. *Richard Utilla*

158

159

159. Plastic dice form handles for cocktail picks and the bowl of an improbable cigarette holder. *Richard Utilla*

160. When the cocktail shaker's cap is twisted open, the plastic face bares its teeth to function as a pouring spout. The ashtray with wavy metal bars anchoring red plastic handles might be a cubist composition. *Richard Utilla*

160

161

162

163

161. The stepped design of this four-inch-high table lighter resembles skyscraper architecture of the 1920s. Made of molded phenolic resin, it works by striking a wand attached to the domed cap against a flint channel on the lighter's side. *Douglas Taylor*

162. Ashtrays of outstanding Art Deco design were molded by Roanoid Ltd., England, in about 1935. Similar examples were included in the World of Art Deco Exhibition of the Minneapolis Institute of Arts in 1971. *Richard Utilla*

163. The "Airtight Velos Bumper Barrel" was made in England as a humidor. Because phenolic resin could be precision molded, the screw-on lid easily fulfilled the airtight claim. *Richard Utilla*

164. A bedside smoking set in amber Catalin includes a candelholder. The "cigarette" atop the box at the right is actually a handle of molded and painted plastic. *Douglas Taylor*

165. Black phenolic ashtrays were designed for the first-class dining room tables of *R.M.S. Queen Mary* in 1934 and manufactured by Roanoid Ltd. of Birmingham, England. The largest, eight inches in diameter, accommodated cigars and pipes. *Richard C. Faber*

166. "The Smoker's Friend," a swiveling Bakelite cigarette box, was made in England. *Galerie Metropole; photo: Osterkorn*

164

165

166

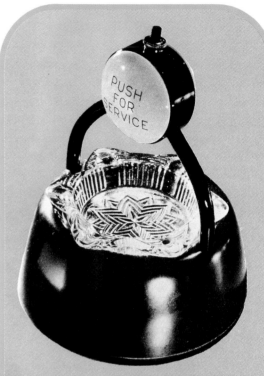

Hey Waiter!

The ultimate restaurant gadget combined a molded plastic ashtray with glass insert and service-call light that could be switched on (in lieu of snapping one's fingers or otherwise signaling) to catch an elusive waiter's eye. Produced by Service Ideas, Inc., in 1953, it was presented to restaurant owners as a money-making device. Service will be speeded up, the inventors claimed, when customers no longer have to struggle to attract their server. They further reasoned, somewhat curiously, that the size of the check may be increased as patrons find it easier to summon the waiter or waitress. Finally, they said, increased service efficiency would result in larger tips. Judging from the rarity of this gizmo, called "Service Boy," it never caught on with either restaurant owners or diners, who evidently preferred to struggle with the traditional, and often futile, fingersnap. *Reprinted from* Durez Plastic News, *November, 1953*

167

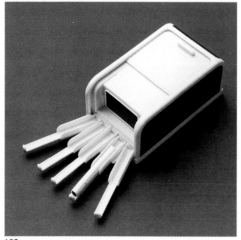

167. A collection of Bakelite ashtrays from Europe and America displays an unusual variety of forms and commercial logos. The green one, lower right, advertises "elephant shelters, tarpaulins and tents" from a London supplier. *Photo: Galerie Roudillon; Christian Gervais*

168. The English-made Rolinx cigarette box thrusts out five "fingers" when the rolltop lid is lifted, each serving up a cigarette. The cream-white plastic is urea-formaldehyde. *Susan Ellsworth*

168

modern look and low price. A consumer survey conducted by the Boymans Museum in preparation for their Bakelite show in 1981 revealed that many people remembered the odd new material as being essentially practical; but no one would think of giving something made of Bakelite as a present because it was too common. And even if the plastic version of the familiar item did offer improvement—a rigid, molded cigar case, for example, was more likely to keep cigars from being crushed than the soft leather variety—a more precious material would still have been preferred for the prestige it carried.

The use of plastic connoted, more than anything else, modernity; and it was in this spirit that the designers of the luxury liner *Queen Mary* adopted plastic materials for the ship's interiors and accessories. It is estimated that over $100,000 worth of plastic was used on the ship in the form of laminate for the walls and also in accessories such as ashtrays for the first-class dining room (on page 123). Sometimes true luxury was evoked by combining plastics with precious metals. For example, a European manufacturer lined a set of phenolic stacking ashtrays with silver.

Fountain Pens

Combinations of plastics with precious materials were, of course, very unusual, except in the fountain pen industry where cellulose nitrate (Celluloid and other brands such as Pyralin and Tenite) had replaced hard rubber in the twenties. Rubber had proved too

169

169. This 8 x 7 inch Art Deco gift box was offered in 1937 by the American Stationery Co. for $.75 with the purchase of their "Big 450" stationery package. Another slightly larger model was available for $1.00. It was designed and molded of phenolic resin by the short-lived plastics division of the Gorham Silver Company that ceased operation in 1940. *J. Harry DuBois*

170. The streamlined "Aristocrat" stapler designed for the E. H. Hotchkiss Company of Norwalk, Conn., by Orlo Heller in 1937 won first prize in that year's *Modern Plastics* magazine competition. The plastic housing made of marbleized phenolic resin resulted in what the Hotchkiss Co. called "the most beautiful stapler in the world."

170

171

172

173

171. Pieces from an amber-toned phenolic desk set were made in England between 1948 and 1951 by John Dickenson and Co., Ltd. The complete "Carvacraft" set includes a double inkwell and a spring-loaded telephone index holder. *Douglas Taylor*

172. The Electro-Pointer pencil sharpener made by Triple "E" Products Co. in 1941 had a formidable black phenolic housing for an automatic motor. The manufacturer claimed it saved more than $100.00 per year in time and pencil waste. *Reprinted from* Durez Plastics News, *October, 1941.*

173. The Rite-O-Way penholder, a good example of classic teardrop streamlining, was made by the Wasp Pen Company, Inc., in 1938. *Reprinted from* Durez Plastics News, *August, 1938.*

brittle and tended to lose its luster. Because fountain pens had always been considered gift items, luxury models were regularly equipped with gold or silver clips, nibs, and trim. Manufacturers chose cellulose nitrate because, as a thermoplastic, it easily could be drawn into the necessary tube shape, and it was resistant to the water, salts, dyes, and drying solvents present in inks. Once formed, the tubes could be finished—the ends tapered and welded

closed—by means of solvents. This could not be done with thermosets such as the phenolic and urea plastics. Also, cellulosic material had an almost unlimited color range.

Pen designers could achieve many decorative variations, such as striping and marbleizing, by crosscutting a block of Celluloid formed from varicolored layers laminated together. Eversharp's Skyliner fountain pen and pencil set, designed in 1941 by Henry Dreyfuss, featured a two-tone striped top with a harmonizing solid-color barrel. A best-seller until well into 1948, the design is thought to have inspired the Swiss-made Mont Blanc and the Italian Columbus pens.

Many pen companies produced desk sets that combined pen holders and inkwell, notepad holders, calendars, letter openers, and blotters. Even more specialized equipment such as staplers and pencil sharpeners came in for updating and sometimes streamlining. In the early forties, for example, the Shaeffer Pen Company hired the industrial designer Thomas Tibbs to "dress up" their pens. Tibbs created smart modern desk sets that included pens and holders and sometimes even lamps in a single unit. Luxury was suggested by combining gleaming black or mottled Bakelite with chrome, just as furniture designers were attempting for tables and desks.

Clocks

Around 1915, the Seth Thomas Clock Company produced an Empire-style desk clock—the Sonora quarter-hour chime—with an "Adamantine" finish (patented in 1885) that was actually

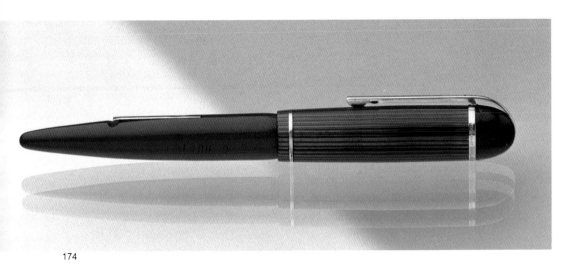

174. The streamlined Skyliner fountain pen designed by Henry Dreyfuss for Eversharp was a bestseller from 1941 to 1948. It was made of Pyroxylin (cellulose nitrate) in a variety of colors and metal combinations including stainless steel and, as shown, 14 karat gold. *The Pen Fanciers Club*

175. Transparent acrylic drafting equipment enabled artists to see the entire drawing surface as they worked. As these c. 1939 Plexiglas examples demonstrate, the result was a beauty derived entirely from form and function. *Photo: Rohm & Haas*

174

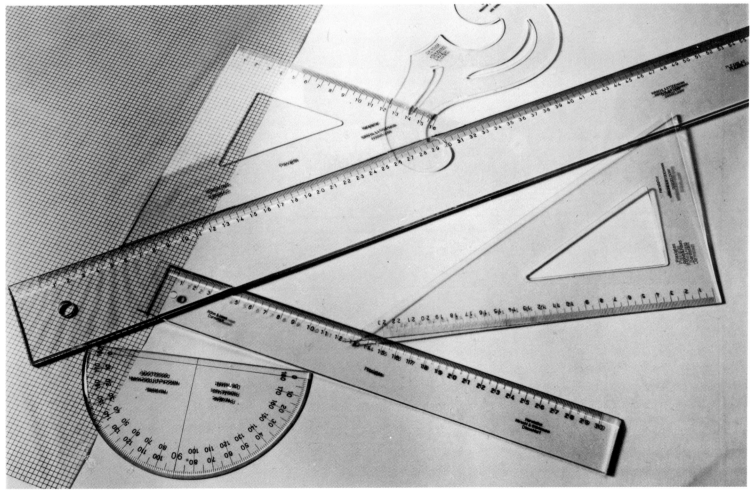

175

176

Celluloid veneer colored to resemble woodgrain. It cost $25.00—not inexpensive then—and was possibly the first use of plastic materials in clock-case design. Since at least the early twenties, novelty manufacturers had been producing small, inexpensive boudoir clocks with simple one-day windup mechanisms in cases formed entirely of Celluloid. These were often sold as part of period-style Celluloid vanity sets. Celluloid really was unsuited to serious

clock-case design due to its fragility, but by the late twenties sturdier Bakelite moldings were offering greater strength, bolder forms, and the possibility of housing electrical mechanisms. In France in the twenties the Jaz Molding Company produced case designs using phenolic resin under the trade name Jazolite. Forms reflected the newly fashionable modern style.

But both in Europe and America clock design was deeply rooted in tra-

ditional styles and materials, mainly wood, brass, and glass; so the clock-making industry yielded slowly and grudgingly to modernization. Concepts of streamlining made an impact in the thirties, but the most dramatically successful redesign story—Henry Dreyfuss's Big Ben alarm clock for Westclox, about 1932—was realized in metal. And though it was modern insofar as it was completely devoid of ornament, in form it was a subliminal echo of old mantel

177

176. French Art Deco clocks with molded phenolic cases that imitated popular wood designs were produced by Jaz and Gautier. *Photo: Galerie Roudillon; Christian Gervais*

177. The case for this four-inch-high Art Deco clock was made from a solid block of Catalin. The works were provided by the Waterbury Clock Company, Conn. *Douglas Taylor*

clock designs that Dreyfuss knew would prove popular with consumers.

A number of American companies did experiment with plastics before World War II to produce colorful and/or streamlined novelties. One of the most common streamlined designs in the U.S. had a ribbed black phenolic case accented with chrome strips. But some manufacturers followed the European example and produced more exotic pyramidal and stepped designs using colorful cast phenolic resins to achieve a more luxurious effect. Some cases of this style were extremely simple in construction: merely a hole bored through a solid block of plastic (this page) to receive a windup mechanism. Others, more elaborate, combined several colors. In 1935, for example, the design firm of J. H. Tyson produced a desk clock with a black and ivory case, a red face, and ivory hands set on a gold flecked clear base. In the same year, Raymond Loewy put ivory plastic numerals on a blue glass clock face with red and gold hands. In 1934, Gilbert Rohde, who produced many beautiful and luxurious modern clock designs for the Herman Miller company in glass, chrome, wood, and leather, used gray Formica and pearlized Celluloid as alternative facing materials for a square slab-face clock set with chrome balls instead of numerals.

The American clock industry, which

Early Desk Phones

The "candlestick" or pedestal phone, top, was considered streamlined in its day, from about 1900 to 1925. Made of cast brass and later steel, it remained standard desk equipment until 1928 when Bell introduced the first handset in which speaking and listening elements were combined in one piece. These were also produced at first in metal, although some phenolic moldings were made in the early thirties. *Photos: Bell Laboratories*

178

had been particularly hard hit by the Depression, was further devastated by World War II. Many companies were forced to shut down entirely for two or three years and convert to war work. Clock-making tools were used to produce fuses for bombs, and other timed instruments. After the war these companies were faced with the enormous task of retooling and refinancing for a new kind of mass production; and many family-owned tradition-bound companies that could not make the adjustment went out of business for good. In addition, the fostering of Japanese and German industries by the United States after the war and the concommitant lowering of import tariffs on foreign goods made it cheaper for American companies to import clockworks from abroad. As a result, many clock-making firms became essentially case-makers. The most inexpensive case was of injection-molded plastic and typically had

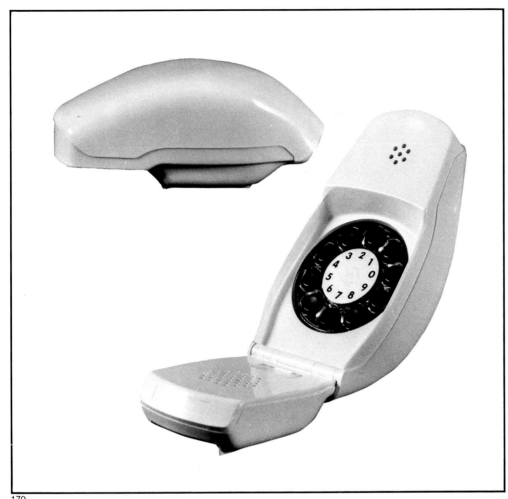

179

178. Henry Dreyfuss's 1937 redesign of Bell Telephone's first handset featured a heavy black phenolic molding. It had many stylistic improvements; but the subsequent 1950 version, produced in lightweight thermoplastic, was more successful in every respect. The hand piece was easier to hold and rested more securely in the cradle. *1937 model, Howard Morris*

179. The *Grillo* (Cricket) folding telephone was designed in 1965 by Marco Zanuso and Richard Sapper for Sit-Siemens (Italy). The ABS plastic housing, only 6½ inches long closed, featured a built-in dial and flip-down mouthpiece. *Museum of Modern Art, New York. Gift of Societa Italiana Telecomunicazioni, Milan.*

as aluminum, brass, and chrome to create modern yet luxurious designs.

The transformation of clocks into kinetic sculptures has always challenged clock-makers. In past centuries, clockworks have been used to animate figures for no other reason than to delight and intrigue the observer. For much the same reasons, contemporary designs have used modern technology to create clocks that operate as light shows or display a high degree of optical engineering. In these designs, actual time-telling is secondary to the visual effects that result from the movement's complexity. Often, plastics, with their clarity and ability to be precision molded into lightweight component parts, play an integral role in the realization of these ingenious and often costly designs. The accuracy of the Helix (page 9), for example, depends on the precision molding of the ABS modules that comprise the ever-turning spiral.

Phones

Until about 1937, the single most jarring note—from a design point of view

few parts—usually a back, a front, and a shatterproof acrylic lens—all of which could be put together quickly to form a dust-free enclosure. By the 1960s electrical and battery-operated plastic clocks were assuming slick organic shapes inspired mostly by Italian designers. (On the other hand, of course, there were the much more prevalent novelty clocks that had graced many a kitchen wall since the late forties. One notable rarity shaped like Al Capp's lovable comic-strip creature the Shmoo was manufactured by Lux of Waterbury, Connecticut, in 1949. It came in white, pink, or blue plastic, featured a 30-hour pendulette movement, and sold for $2.98.)

Among the many plastics available to designers, acrylic, for its optical clarity, and ABS, for its gloss and color spectrum, have been most often preferred. In addition, these plastics can be used effectively with metals such

180. Three of the earliest plastic cameras include, right, the c. 1927 Kodak Hawkette from England, center, the German-made Ebner, rare and valuable with streamlined case, introduced in Stuttgart in 1934; and the American Q.R.S. Kamra, a full-frame fixed-focus 35mm with uncommon box shape and horizontally oriented viewfinder. All are molded of Bakelite, but the unusual mottling of the Q.R.S. was achieved with a filler of canvas fiber. *All cameras except Figure 184 from the collection of Eaton S. Lothrop, Jr.*

180

—on the modernized desktop would have been the telephone. Although the Bell Telephone Company had developed its own handset—a modernization of the old candlestick model—as early as 1927, the bulbous design was clumsy and heavy. To accomplish an overhaul, Bell hired Henry Dreyfuss, then a young, aspiring industrial designer, to provide "a little art to wrap the telephone in." Dreyfuss characteristically insisted on a total approach to the phone's redesign and spent hours with Bell's engineers in an effort to improve the inner workings as well as the outward appearance of the instrument.

Dreyfuss's 1937 model, like Bell's first handset, was produced in molded black phenolic resin, which was nonetheless quite heavy. The handpiece with its high, ridged back was difficult to hold and easily displaced off the hook. Also, there was no way to regulate the volume of the ring, and the dial face, placed directly under the dial

holes, was difficult to clean. In 1950, Dreyfuss again redesigned the phone using a lightweight thermoplastic for the housing that is still common in most American homes. A more radical design solution to the problems of compactness and receiver-off-the-hook syndrome was offered by L. M. Ericsson of Stockholm, whose one-piece phone with dial and switch-button in the base vaguely resembled a seated giraffe. Its function was obvious, however, unlike the Grillo or "Cricket" folding phone designed in 1967 by Italians Marco Zanuso and Richard Sapper. In closed position, it resembled the sleek white carapace of an insect while giving no indication of its function. Such playfulness, characteristic of postwar Italian design in general, inadvertently may have provoked the fun-phone craze. It is also possible that the designers were merely giving expression to an Italian proverb, "*indovinalo grillo*," which cryptically translates as "the cricket has the secret."

Photographic Equipment

For collectors of photographica who normally look for equipment that represents technological landmarks, plastic cameras represent a nostalgic diversion into the essentially superficial area of case design. In the thirties, dozens of companies in the U.S. and abroad began to produce cheap basic cameras molded in sturdy phenolic resin in answer to the demand of the growing hoards of amateur photographers. They sold for as little as 49 cents up to a couple of dollars; and most offered no improvement over the first Brownie introduced by Kodak in 1900 for one dollar. These were point-and-shoot cameras that, like today's Instamatic, required no focusing. Both for Kodak, undisputed leader in the field, and other smaller firms, such simplicity sheathed in a shiny molded black case spelled profit to a phenomenal degree. Kodak's Baby Brownie, with its case designed in 1934 by Walter Dorwin Teague, reportedly sold four million at a dollar a

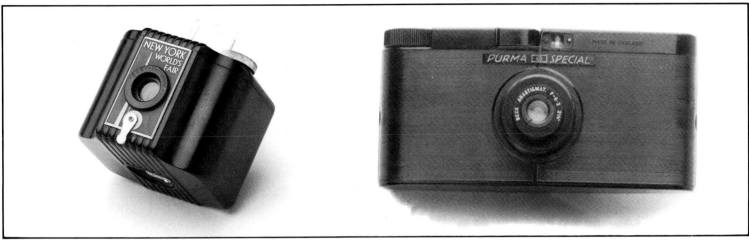

181

182

183

184

181. Cameras by leading American industrial designers include, left, Kodak's Baby Brownie dollar camera with case by Walter Dorwin Teague. Although millions were sold, this version with a World's Fair faceplate is slightly rarer than earlier models. Raymond Loewy's Purma Special, right, was designed for Purma Cameras, Ltd., England, in 1937. It had an acrylic viewfinder lens and a gravity-controlled focal-plane shutter invented by A. D. Mayo.

182. The $12.95 Argus Model A, introduced in 1936 by International Research Corp., was described as the first precision-made 35mm camera in America at an affordable price. It had a sturdy, molded plastic case and quality lens with shutter speeds up to 1/200 of a second.

183. The Russian *Shkolnik* (Schoolboy) camera, probably made after World War II, has an ungainly bulbous case design and is technically simplistic.

184. At least a million of these tiny plastic Univex cameras were sold for $1.00 each at the 1933 Chicago World's Fair. Made by the Universal Camera Corp., they used "Univex No. 00 Film Rolls Only" and were "equipped with Special Univex synchronomatic Speedlens." *J. Harry DuBois*

185

186

187

piece. Teague's little black box with its distinctive vertical ribbing did not, however, represent Kodak's first use of plastic. In England, in 1927, the company had produced the Hawkette, a folding pocket camera of standard design, in mottled Bakelite, and that may have been the first plastic camera ever made.

Argus, one of Kodak's major competitors, produced several plastic cameras in the thirties, some of which were

185. Cameras from the late 1950s and early '60s include the Zeiss Ikonette, left, a 35mm camera whose styling was meant to appeal to women; and the Kodak Brownie Vecta whose easy-grip case had a depression on top for the thumb.

186. The colorful Ferrania 3M is an Italian-made Instamatic from the late 1960s.

187. "Personality" cameras marketed in the 1950s for young people featured comic character labels for the glamorous red-haired reporter Brenda Starr, Dick Tracy, and Hopalong Cassidy.

a bit more complex than the Brownie-type. The Argus Model A, for example, was offered as the first popularly priced —at $12.95—"All American precision-made 35mm miniature camera." The Argoflex boasted "ground glass focusing and two fast F:4.5 lenses." The Purma Special, designed by Raymond Loewy for Purma Cameras, Ltd., in England, offered the intriguing innovations of a perspex (acrylic) viewfinder lens and three-speed focal-plane shutter that worked by gravity according to the position in which the camera was held!

Undoubtedly the cheapest and smallest plastic camera ever produced was the 35mm Univex A (page 133) that sold for 39 cents or was given away as a premium from 1933 to 1937. Its distinctive feature—it would take only special Universal film at six shots for a dollar— proved popular with consumers who bought over 22 million rolls. The profits were plowed back into the company, Universal Camera Corp.,

188. Character cameras for children include, from the top, a Bugs Bunny instant-load from 1977; a Mick-a-matic produced by Child Guidance Products in 1969; a contemporary Smurf camera; and a Snoopy-matic by Helm Toy Corp. from 1976. The ten-inch-high Charlie Tuna camera was a premium offered by Star-Kist Foods, Inc., in 1972 and is now rare.

which developed several quality 35mm cameras and optical instruments until it went bankrupt in 1952.

Because plastic cameras were so cheap to produce, they were heavily promoted for the children's market. (The Brownie and Buster Brown cameras of 1900 had been made of cardboard.) In the fifties, American manufacturers produced a line of "personality" cameras that bore labels around the lens identifying them with Brenda Starr, Dick Tracy, and Hopalong Cassidy (page 134). And in 1969 the Mick-a-matic, in the shape of Mickey Mouse's head, was introduced by Child Guidance Products. In an early version, quickly discontinued, Mickey's right ear acted as the shutter release, but this feature did not appeal to kids.

Probably because photographic equipment was put away when not in use, relatively little importance was placed on outward stylistic variations. However, for radios, which were constantly on view in the home, case de-

sign became one of the most significant merchandising efforts of the decade, particularly as concerns the use of plastic.

Radios

Between 1920 and 1927, annual sales of radio receivers rose from some $2 million to $136 million. This increase reflected the phenomenal growth of public broadcasting, which also can be viewed in terms of the growth in numbers of stations during that same period. In 1920 there were three radio stations in America; in 1927 there were 800. Around 1931, radio as a public broadcasting medium had spread all over the world, and America was launching radio's Golden Age with great performers and shows such as Rudy Vallee, Amos and Andy, and The Goldbergs, whose services, not insignificantly, were paid for out of advertising revenues. Radio thrived during the Depression when it was the one unifying spark of vitality and source of

189. These Fada radios date from about 1934, when the company went out of business under that name. Desirable for their streamlined forms, plastic Fadas are also prized for their richly colored cast phenolic cases. *Dennis J. O'Donnell*

". . . and it comes out here."

In the twenties, plastics figured significantly in the forward-thinking marketing strategies of the Philips Corporation, Holland's foremost electronics firm. The Philips radio loudspeaker, Type 2003, right, was made in the Netherlands in 1925 of molded Bakelite (called Philite by the company). Nineteen-inches high, it was at the time the largest molding being produced anywhere and was consciously designed as an "art object" to enhance marketability. By the early thirties, Philips was producing many decorative variations, as shown below. In each case, color and forms were carefully developed to appeal to different economic and social levels within Philips' European marketplace. *Photos: Galerie Roudillon, Paris; Christian Gervais*

190

191

190. This was the first plastic radio offered by Sears, in 1936, for $12.50. The brown phenolic case with ivory and brown dial, had an unusual wraparound grille that gave the set a finished look when viewed from either front or back. *Reprinted from* Durez Plastics News, *June-July, 1936*

191. The 1937 Pilot radio, 18½ inches high, was the largest plastic radio cabinet made in that year. Designed by Jan Streng for the export market, it had a sturdy one-piece molded case that alone weighed ten pounds and could, according to the manufacturer, withstand the weight of a man without breaking. *Reprinted from* Durez Plastics News, *August-September, 1937*

amusement available to everyone— from a sharecropper to a Rockefeller. Not everyone had a telephone, but (almost) everyone had a radio. In the early years of broadcasting, programming was supplied by the companies who had developed the technolgy and who owned the stations. They also manufactured the receivers and sets, realizing that if they were going to sell radios they had to provide the public with something worthwhile to listen to—free

of charge. Therefore, corporations such as Westinghouse, RCA, and General Electric became pioneers of the creative arm of the industry.

The earliest sets were large pieces of wooden parlor furniture with hand-built wooden cabinets that often resembled little Gothic cathedrals. A deluxe radio could cost several hundred dollars in the late twenties; a moderately priced one about $50.00. Plastics, when they entered the market

during the Depression, brought prices down to as low as $9.95 for a "midget" that might be as small as six inches wide. The Depression and the popularity of radio broadcasting provided the plastics industry with optimum conditions for cornering a significant portion of the market. (American manufacturers were late in seeing the potential of plastics. As early as 1925, the Dutch electronics company Philips had begun to produce spectacular loudspeakers

192

193

194

192. The stylish Belmont radio from 1946 featured push-button tuning, a side tuning knob, and a gleaming white spray-bake finish over a black phenolic case. *Reprinted from* Durez Plastics News, *August, 1946*

193. The prominent industrial design firm of Barnes and Reinecke created this "Topper" model for the Kadette Radio Corp. in 1940. It was one of the most unusual prewar designs, with its cone-shaped speaker that dispersed sound 360° in an early attempt at acoustical engineering. *Reprinted from* Durez Plastics News, *September, 1940*

194. An elegant Philco table radio from 1949 has a white-lacquered finish. The dial is maroon, green, and copper with gold numerals. *Dennis J. O'Donnell*

in Bakelite, or Philite, as they called it, that were used in conjunction with the earliest consumer radios. Philips designed them as "art objects" [page 137] to appeal to an audience with refined tastes.) In 1939, *Communications*, a radio industry trade publication released sales figures of table model radios for the first six months of the year and for 1937 and 1938. Plastic cabinets represented a major percentage of total sales in each year. In

1938, for example, of a total of 5,880,000 sets sold, 1,420,000 were plastic. These figures reflected the production of dozens of companies and a staggering variety of designs.

Designers were under pressure to make frequent style changes in order to compete in the market and to keep the lines looking up-to-date. In the rush, they often engaged in battle with mold engineers who complained that certain types of designs were unsuited to mold-

OVERLEAF:

195. An unusual round radio designed in 1935 by Wells Coates for E. K. Cole, Ltd., had a mottled phenolic case. *Photo: Galerie Roudillon; Christian Gervais*

196. The Ekco SH25 Superhet Wireless radio, designed in 1932 by E. K. Cole Ltd., had one of the most decorative phenolic cases, with a grille patterned after a landscape. *Photo: from Sylvia Katz; Crown Copyright Victoria and Albert Museum*

197

197. A very unusual cabinet radio from the 1930s has doors, as well as case, of molded Bakelite. Sixteen inches high, with white knobs and wooden ball feet painted white, it is marked only "Siemens" and is possibly Austrian. *Galerie Metropol; photo: Osterkorn*

ing and produced weak products that cracked easily. Particularly susceptible to cracking, if the wall thickness of the plastic was not adequate, were the louvers, or vents. In other instances, when the casing was too small to accommodate the tubes, the set could overheat and cause the plastic to shrink, crack, or discolor if light-colored urea plastic was used. Eventually engineers developed techniques for making minor changes in the molds so that models could be varied from season to season without having to write off the entire cost of the expensive steel mold each time.

At first, plastic radio designers attempted to imitate the Gothic style of the old wooden cabinets, but the pointed arches and ornate relief patterns proved incompatible to molding techniques. Instead, rounded edges and plain surfaces prevailed and designs for the most part became horizontal. One interesting exception was the skyscraper radio designed by Harold Van Doren and John Gordon Rideout for Air King Products Company in 1933. It was one of the few to display vertical Art Deco—as opposed to streamlined—styling.

Writing in *Modern Plastics* magazine in 1936, Franklin E. Brill, of General Plastics, Inc., one of the largest molders in the country, reported that Sears, Roebuck "has put its official stamp of approval on plastics for radio cabinets" with the introduction of the Silvertone compact designed by John Morgan. "Now that the Modernistic versus Gothic question has been definitely settled," said Brill, "and cabinet design has stabilized into a clean, but not stark-looking modern technique, plas-

tic materials have come into their own in radio cabinet work." Like most of the plastic radios of the 1930s, the first Silvertone was molded of phenolic resin in black and brown; but designers realized that color was their biggest selling point and tried to dress up the dark cases by using contrasting grille cloth and knobs or dials in light-colored urea plastic. As the decade progressed, more and more radios were being produced in white or cream-colored urea moldings or in dark phenolics spray-lacquered white, an effective process that could transform a fairly workaday model into an elegant living room accessory.

The most expensive plastic radios were those produced in the glowing jewel-like colors of cast phenolic resin. They rarely sold for under $15.00, while the dark, molded phenolics generally could be had for $10.00 or less. This was because the casting process was essentially more labor-intensive and incapable of the same high-volume production as high-pressure molding in which a typical production run was 100,000. Cast phenolic cabinets were formed by pouring the viscous phenolic syrup into lead molds. The castings were then placed in ovens to bake, or cure, for about three days. They then were removed as rough castings and hand-polished. The lead molds were used only once for each casting and melted down. These radios retain their colors over the decades and are the most popular with American collectors.

Extreme examples of streamlining were surprisingly rare in radio design. In a 1939 roundup of plastic cabinets, *Durez Plastics News* presented its read-

198

199

200

ers with a variety of design treatments from various manufacturers that they felt revealed a conservative streamlined trend. "All are very modern, yet none bizarre as they well might be in our present tear-drop stage of streamlining." Indeed, one of the most unusual designs was the Kadette "Topper," created for the Kadette Radio Corporation by the industrial design firm of Barnes and Reinecke in 1940. Essentially a box mounted with a raised, circular, cone-topped speaker that supposedly dispersed sound throughout a full 360° swing, the design won high honors in the fifth annual Modern Plastics Competition.

Television

With the advent of television in the late 1940s, molders naturally tackled the problems inherent in producing the necessarily larger one-piece cabinet molding by the same means used for

198. Philco's "People's set" from 1935 was one of the most common radios produced in England. *Photo: Galerie Roudillon; Christian Gervais*

199. An Emerson portable radio from the early 1950s predates transistors but is, nonetheless, surprisingly small, only 7½ inches wide. Collectors appreciate the graphic quality of the case design. *Dennis J. O'Donnell*

200. Braun's T3 pocket-sized transistor radio produced in 1958 was one of the first of its kind. The minimalist styling rendered in light-gray thermoplastic was the antithesis of Depression-era compression-molded case design. *Photo: Braun AG*

Phonographs

By the late twenties, phonograph cases were being produced in plastic. Many of them were portables, such as the 12-inch Philips player, shown above, that packs up into a Bakelite case resembling a hatbox—a rarity today. During the fifties, however, molded phenolic cases became more common, and many housed radio-phonograph combinations in their streamlined design. The 1951 Admiral, below, is valued more for its styling than for the quality of its fairly crude electronics. *Photos: top, Galerie Metropole; below, David Arky*

small radio cabinets—high compression molding. In 1949 an article in *Modern Plastics* explained that a wood "consolette-type" cabinet required 525 different construction operations before the chassis could be installed; a plastic cabinet only required from three to six operations. This, and the fact that production runs for molded cabinets would be much faster, contributed to the reduced cost of plastic cabinets, as much as $100 below that of wooden sets. But the mold-making apparatus required to produce a modest little TV cabinet, about 36 inches high and accommodating a 10-inch viewing tube, was awesome. The Admiral Corporation gambled, according to the company, nearly a quarter of a million dollars in tools, dies, and a two-story molding press that is a story in itself.

Admiral decided to make use of a 30-foot-high compression molding press built by Bethlehem Steel for the Russian government. For reasons unknown, the Russians never picked it up. The Molded Products Corporation of Chicago purchased it from an Akron, Ohio, machinery dealer and had it shipped piecemeal to Chicago where it was reassembled. Weighing about 250,000 pounds, it was sunk seven feet beneath the basement floor in a concrete foundation, but still it towered above the roof of the plant; so a penthouse had to be built to accommodate it. The press required a 75 horsepower motor to operate its oil pump, which delivered 2,000 tons, or 4,000,000 pounds, of pressure to each individual molding. To withstand this amount of pressure, the two-part mold was constructed of case-hardened steel with walls 9 to 10 inches

thick and in itself weighed 20,000 pounds. To form a TV cabinet, about 35 pounds of "bricks" of phenolic material were loaded into the mold, which was then heated. The top plunger-half of the mold then descended into the die cavity forcing the molding materials to flow evenly into every crevice. The plunger remained in place for about three-and-a-half minutes, during which time the resin polymerized into an infusible thermoset. When the plunger was lifted it brought the finished cabinet with it. The entire cycle took about seven minutes and could be repeated many times a day. Admiral reported that "sales took a sharp upward curve" with the introduction of this cabinet; the set sold for $249.95 in 1949.

This method also was used in the creation of one-piece molded cabinets for phonographs made by Admiral and others; but by the mid-fifties, with the miniaturization of electronics—principally the elimination of tubes—cabinet design for all types of electronics changed radically. Postwar designers de-emphasized "styling" as it had been so well understood (perhaps too well) in the 1930s and '40s. The earliest portable transistor radios produced by Braun in Germany, for example, were so extremely spare and subtle they seemed ascetic compared to the bold curvy Bakelite models of the Depression. The Braun approach, which they carried over most successfully into their appliance line, ushered in a new era of industrial design in which electronic equipment would undergo unparalleled refinement, both in the use of plastics and, of course, in the technology itself.

201

201–202. A press two-stories high, capable of exerting 2,000 tons of pressure, was required to form a 36-inch-high Admiral television cabinet, using phenolic resin, in 1949. *Reprinted from* Durez Plastics News, *June, 1949.*

202

4   PLAYTHINGS

"Toyland has opened its frontiers wide to the machine age." *Toy World*, 1935

In November of 1939, more than one month after the outbreak of war in Europe and one month before Christmas, a German cargo ship unloaded 1,200 tons of toys in New York. That the ship had been allowed passage at all was an extraordinary event. But German toy manufacturers had appealed to the government, who had permitted shipment through Holland. This was the

203. This teenager's desk is a treasure trove of contemporary plastic toys and novelties. In the foreground are small windup toys from Hong Kong, including two red crabs, a blue hippo, and a robot. The music box, far right, with automated clown on a bicycle, is all plastic, as is the inflatable robot, top right, and acrylic parrot lamp, left. Other plastics include a zany drinking straw and waterproof song book for the shower. Retractable high-tech scissors are made in Japan. Plastic beer glasses printed with names of various colleges are popular souvenirs among young people. *Messy desk, Anna Rawls; with additions from author's collection.*

last batch of German-made toys that American children would enjoy for many Christmases to come, and it was the beginning of an austere period for American toy makers, who found themselves bereft not only of crucial imports but of equally crucial materials as basic as boxes in which to ship their products to dealers. In 1945, *Toys and Novelties* magazine praised manufacturers for the ingenuity they had displayed in securing materials: "The lumber situation at one time was appalling, and more than one toy manufacturer had to suspend the wooden toy end of his business, but he produced plastic or paperboard toys, and kept the wheels of the industry turning!"

Hiram McCann, then the associate publisher of *Modern Plastics* magazine, estimated that plastic represented 25 percent of the toy market in 1946 when total sales were over $160 million. However, the children born in the early 1940s were not the first generation to have plastic toys to play with.

Toys were among the first objects produced by 19th-century Celluloid

204

205

manufacturers. Baby toys, tub toys (some little boats could be propelled by the bubbling action of camphor in water), and dolls—including jointed dolls with real hair—were being made as early as 1880; and Kewpie dolls were sold by Sears, Roebuck after 1911. Celluloid could not have been more inappropriate as a toy material. Not only was it much too fragile and easily punctured but it was, of course, extremely flammable due to the presence of nitrates—a common explosive ingredient—in its composition. These factors account for the scarcity of these toys today and the Celluloids made briefly in Occupied Japan after World War II. Celluloid eventually was banned as an unsafe material and still should be handled with care by collectors. Never expose celluloid to direct heat.

Traditionally, toys were made of wood, tin, cast iron, cloth, bisque (china), and paper. The use of modern plastics, apart from Celluloid, did not begin until the late 1930s when many children encountered them for the first time in the form of radio premiums— Lone Ranger rings and such. Some children had their own plastic radios that could resemble toys. There were, for example, radios that included molded figures of Edgar Bergen's ventriloquist dummy Charlie McCarthy, the Dionne quintuplets, and Mickey Mouse. But a toy such as a molded plastic ocarina or bubble pipe would have impressed kids and their parents as being very modern indeed. In 1939, at the New York World's Fair, a plastic toy bank shaped like an American transport plane was considered an unusual souvenir.

204. Fragile Celluloid tub toys date from the first decade of the century. *Linda Campbell Franklin*

205–206. Celluloid Disney toys made in Japan in the 1930s are among the most valuable plastics. The six-inch-long tub toy featuring Mickey Mouse, above, sold at auction for $1175.00 in 1981. The Celluloid and tin windup toy, opposite, features Donald Duck at the center of a spinning carousel from which other Disney characters are suspended. It sold at auction in 1981 for $950.00. The high prices reflect both rarity and the enthusiasm of Disneyana collectors. *Photos: Lloyd Ralston Toy Auction*

207. Crib toys from the 1930s are made of Catalin. *Douglas Taylor*

206

207

208

209

Even streamlined toys, one of the most fascinating of phenomena in toy history, were rarely made of plastic. Designed mainly during the thirties and forties, they comprised mostly pedal cars, tricycles, and coasters made of cast metal, wearing, as *Toy World* magazine put it in 1935, "airplane 'pants' over their wheels or their runners." Child-sized appliances such as the "Little Miss Streamlined" toy carpet sweeper were also made as exact replicas of mother's. Mother's probably *was* made of plastic.

By the late forties and early fifties, a few streamlined toy vehicles were being produced in plastic but never in large numbers. (As late as 1954 at the American Toy Fair in New York, the Inland Manufacturing Corporation of Buffalo, New York, displayed a prototype for a streamlined pedal car made of fiberglass-reinforced plastic, the material then in use primarily for boat hulls. The

208. A model racing car manufactured by Reuhl Products in 1949 had a miniature gasoline engine and could attain speeds of more than 100 miles per hour. The body was molded of phenolic resin reinforced with fiberglass and wood flour. Frame and axles are of cast aluminum. *Reprinted from* Durez Plastics News, *May, 1949.*

209. A rare miniature car of molded Bakelite was probably manufactured in Austria in the 1930s. *Galerie Metropole; photo: Osterkorn*

210. A magazine advertisement from 1946 promotes the streamlined Tuffy Traveler as "the automobile of tomorrow." Like many life-sized prototypes developed during the late 1930s, the toy had only three wheels.

The automobile of tomorrow. Plastic body. Variety of color. Motor space in the rear. Luggage space in front. Transparent top removable. Clear headlight lens. No fenders. Bumpers all around. Spare tire. Metal axle. Plastic steering wheel. The individual box is "The Garage." 3¼ inches wide — 2¾ inches high and 7¾ inches long. Packed 3 and 2 dozen per carton — Shipping weight respectively 15 and 10 pounds.

210

211–212. The make, origin, and manufacturer of this sleek two-toned sedan is unknown, but the colors—mauve and chartreuse—suggest the 1950s. The trucks, below, illustrate the much-bolder colors made possible by polystyrene in the fifties. *Dennis J. O'Donnell*

213.

214

215

213. A miniature toy reproduction of Russel Wright's famous "American Modern" ceramicware was produced in polystyrene by the Ideal Toy Co. in 1955. *Robert Shaw*

214. A Tupperware school kit in "safety yellow" was designed to insure high visibility for the child carrying it. Made with an integrally molded handle, it is hinged at the base and lies flat when opened. *Photo: Tupperware*

215. The Campbell Soup Company offered this plastic cup as a premium in the early 1980s as a soup bowl for kids. *Linda Campbell Franklin*

"X-9 Super Jet" had three wheels in classic streamlined style and was 55 inches long with a fuselage nose cone, high vertical tail fin, and aircraft control panel in imitation of wartime aircraft. It weighed only 35 pounds, much less than cast-steel cars made in early decades. Its manufacturing history is unknown.)

After 1939, toy manufacturers began to experiment with the colorful thermo-setting urea-formaldehyde plastics that could be sterilized and had smooth nonallergenic surfaces to produce all sorts of baby toys. Rattles, teethers, and cradle gyms were most common. But those who were young parents at the time recall that these plastics often cracked and seemed insubstantial in comparison to what later became available for their grandchildren. Newly developed vinyl was coming into use for the manufacture of dolls because it provided a lifelike imitation of skin. And, increasingly, polystyrene and poly-ethylene, both tough thermoplastics,

216

were being used for brightly colored heavy-use toys such as vehicles and wagons. Sales records for particular items forced manufacturers to consider the implications of plastics for the future of the industry: in the late forties, as reported in *Toys and Novelties*, Ideal's toy plastic telephone sold over 3 million in three years; Universal Plastics Corporation sold more than a third-of-a-million plastic trombones in less than a year. And little girls' tea sets, made by various manufacturers, sold over 2.5 million between 1953 and 1956. One of the best sellers in this last category was the pint-sized version of Russel Wright's famous American Modern ceramic dinnerware produced in polystyrene by Ideal in the 1950s.

It was not as if similar toys had not existed before, but they never had been available at such a low price, a factor attributable to the injection-molding process. All the parts for a toy vehicle

216. Injection-molded plastic trains have a high degree of realism while remaining light in weight. Although scaled down to model size, every rivet is accounted for, as are other pieces of important hardware such as ladder, steps, roof, and wheel details. *Walton Rawls*

could be formed in less than a minute in a multicavity mold that could produce about 600 moldings in an hour. This meant that the manufacturer could price the resulting toy, such as the extremely realistic little army jeeps made by Ideal in the fifties, at about 35 cents.

Trains

In the special and venerable area of model trains where realism is valued above all else, plastics contributed more than simply reduced cost. Before 1950, both the A. C. Gilbert Company and the Lionel Corporation had begun to use plastic for both cars and accessories. Both companies found they could achieve great detailing through molding, but the reduced overall weight of the cars permitted more to be added to each set. In August of 1946, Marshall Frisbee, chief engineer for A. C. Gilbert, explained in *Modern Plastics* that "A plastic car weighs one-third as much as the old die-cast car, and instead of a six- or seven-car train the new American Flyer now pulls 14 or 15 cars. The result is greater realism in the length of the train itself. What enthusiast, young or old, does not get a greater thrill from a 10-foot-long train than from one only four feet long?" Also, Frisbee explained, plastic wheels better simulate the click-click of the sound of a real train.

In the late sixties, Lehmann, the century-old German toy firm, found that plastic made it possible to produce a large gauge (G) train that could be set up outdoors in any kind of weather, including snow. This exciting feature, possible only because of nonrusting plastic parts, further heightens the illu-

217

sion of reality by allowing children (and adults—it goes without saying) to play with magnificent, finely detailed, over-sized model trains in a natural setting.

Model Kits

But plastics had their greatest impact around 1950 in the hobby field, specifically in kit-building. The do-it-yourself craze has been attributed to several factors including an irrepressible urge to make things by hand; but in the

immediate postwar years it was fueled by increased leisure time and discretionary income. Model-making, a centuries-old adult activity, had traditionally concerned itself with the exacting recreation of classic ships and vehicles in wood, metal, and other natural materials. Kits could be fairly expensive since they might contain hundreds of tiny parts that were costly to produce. The hobby industry sensed an increased demand for kits after the war,

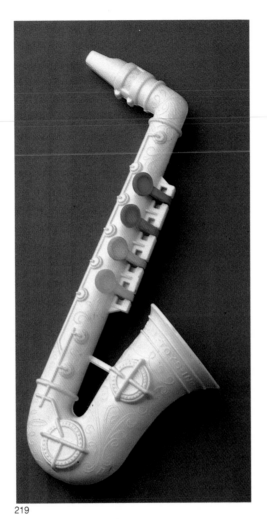

217. A toy electric organ, seven inches high with Bakelite case, was made in the 1940s or '50s by the Magnus Harmonica Corp. of Newark, N.J. *Linda Campbell Franklin*

218. A ten-inch-long Celluloid violin with metal strings was made by the Airfix Company of England. *Clock Tower Antiques, Edgartown, Mass.*

219. A working 10-inch-high saxophone molded with a fancy scroll pattern was produced by Proll Toys, Inc., of Newark, N.J. *Joan Baren*

218

219

and in turning to plastics discovered that through injection-molding they could get good detailing—a fact the model train people had discovered—plus low-cost mass-production of tiny parts.

In the late 1940s, the Revell Company introduced a pull-toy in the form of the Maxwell automobile that Jack Benny made famous on his radio show. Someone suggested that it be revamped as a kit; so Revell tried it with

a kit line of "Highway Pioneers" that sold for 69 cents each, a price well within the reach of most youngsters. They responded eagerly, and the company went on to develop many more.

In the fifties and sixties, many realistic World War II airplane model kits were produced in plastic. If found unbuilt and in unopened boxes, such kits can be very valuable to collectors today. Once put together, however, they tend to be considered just another toy. Writing in

Private Pilot magazine, the toy plane collector K. O. Eckland reported that the Beech Staggerwing kit produced in the mid-sixties for $3.95 was bringing about $60.00 fifteen years later.

After the demonstrated success of plastic in the hobby field, the toy industry began turning to it with increased enthusiasm. By 1980, as *Chemical Week* reported, the toy industry was annually consuming two percent (about 20 million pounds) of all the plastic

220

220. The "Crawlalligator" designed for Creative Playthings in about 1968 was a good exercise toy. It permitted a child to propel himself alligator-style while supported by the 18 x 40 inch polyethylene form mounted on swiveling casters. *Photo: Ferdinand Boesch, from "Plastic as Plastic," American Craft Museum of the American Craft Council, 1968-69.*

produced in the U.S. Polyethylene had the biggest share of the market because of its good safety record, its nontoxicity, and the fact that it did not form sharp edges when broken. Polystyrene had the second biggest share due to its faster molding cycles, greater rigidity, high tensile strength, and gloss. In the doll industry, however, vinyl has remained the preferred material because of its ability to simulate lifelike skin.

Dolls

In a short-lived experiment in 1940, the first "Magic Skin" doll was made of natural rubber; however, vinyl quickly replaced that material because it was tougher and, unlike rubber, did not darken with age. And as in other areas of toy manufacture, vinyl made possible extremely realistic detailing in the modeling of heads and extremities. Plastic heads also could be perforated

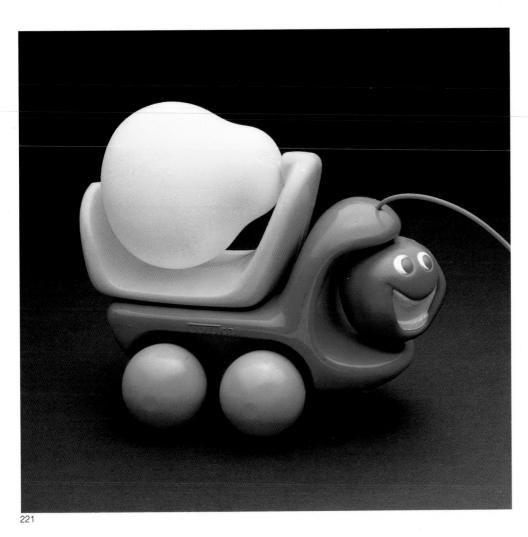

221

222

to accommodate rooted hair; and molded bodies were easily fitted with tubing and mechanisms that enabled the dolls to drink, wet, cry, giggle, sneeze, walk, and, in some cases, sing songs.

The method for making soft realistic baby dolls, possessing what the doll manufacturers call the "huggability factor," was described in a 1976 field report from Mobay Chemical, a lead-ing producer of polyurethane foam. The report described how Kenner Products' "Baby Alive" did in fact come to life: First, a thin vinyl skin was slush molded, a technique in which the milky liquid plastic is made to coat the inside of the mold, thus forming a "skin." The skin was then removed, fitted with tubes and other functional parts and placed in a two-piece fiberglass box mold with a cavity precisely conforming to the doll's

221. A pull-toy by Tonka exhibits the wacky potential of plastics. *Author's collection*

222. A yo-yo made of mottled Bakelite is marked "Regal P.D.C." *Photo: Galerie Roudillon; Christian Gervais*

body. This mold supported the skin as the foaming polyurethane chemicals were introduced. The resilient foam set up instantly, filling every crevice of the skin and inflating the doll's body to soft realistic dimensions. In actual fact, "Baby Alive" was fairly hard-bodied, according to Kenner Products, who, like many other manufacturers, are continually improving on "huggability."

Contemporary baby dolls tend to have a thicker, yet soft, skin that is not always foam-filled. Effanbee, the oldest doll manufacturer in the U.S., claims to be the only firm that stuffs the arms and legs of soft-bodied baby dolls, a feature that they say improves durability and gives it a more realistic feel.

Since the seventies, when OPEC oil crises sent resin prices skyward, less expensive vinyl derivatives have been widely adopted throughout the doll industry, a development that did not seem to have an adverse effect on the quality doll market, where modeling and surface texture of the doll's skin has become more and more appealing and lifelike. In several cases, the artistry of some vinyl dolls begins to rival the beauty of the antique bisque-headed creations that are the aristocracy of dolldom. Effanbee's "Baby Lisa," though a vinyl replica of Astry Campbell's bisque doll in the Smithsonian's collection, is exquisite in its own right.

While the majority of collectors, who belong to 6,000 doll clubs organized nationwide, specialize in antique dolls, many who can no longer afford bisques have turned to vinyls. For the investment-minded, some categories have proven profitability. Among the most favored are the traditionally pretty and

224

lavishly costumed Madame Alexander dolls that have been produced in America since the twenties. With frequent model changes and rigidly controlled distribution, the Alexander organization insures the type of scarcity that creates collectibility. A Jenny Lind doll that sold for $25.00 in 1970 brought $500.00 ten years later, an increase that is not unusual among Alexanders. In 1982, 175 Alexanders sold at auction for $25,000, $15,000 over estimate. A number of doll manufacturers have responded to collecting fever by instituting limited edition artist-designed dolls especially for collectors. Effanbee's Legend series introduced in 1980, for example, offers doll-sized versions of famous personalities such as W. C. Fields, Groucho Marx, John Wayne, and American presidents.

Among the dolls in regular, unlimited, production, none has proved as phenomenally successful as Barbie, the glamorous, curvaceous teenager introduced by Mattel in 1959. Twenty million had been sold by 1980, many to

FACING PAGE:
223. Three generations of plastic dolls include the big-eyed Celluloid Kewpie, front and center, dating from about 1910 and missing arms and legs. The yellow Celluloid Kewpie-inspired baby doll to her right was made in Japan in the 1940s. The others, one child's collection from the early seventies, are inexpensive hard-bodied vinyls including the Shirley Temple doll, possibly the most consistently popular image for dollmakers since the thirties. *Celluloids, author's collection; vinyls, Anna Rawls*

224. The Barbie Doll, as it was introduced by Mattel in 1958, had a curvaceous 11½ inch-high body molded of hard vinyl and an extensive wardrobe. It received an initial cool reception from toy buyers, but by 1980 20 million had been sold. *Photo: Mattel*

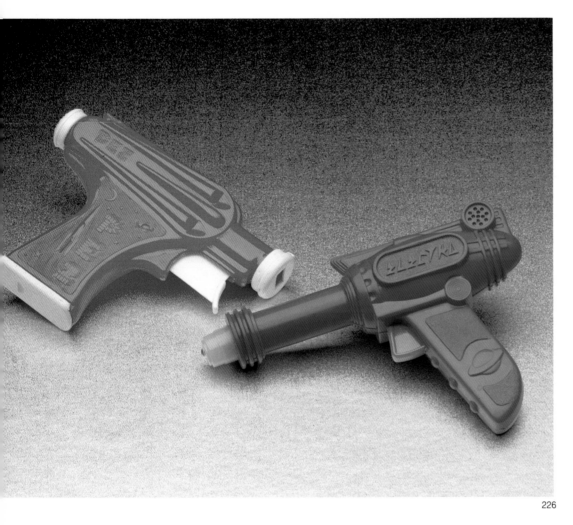

225. Soft-bodied, realistically modeled vinyl dolls such as Effanbee's Baby Lisa have introduced a high level of quality and design to the plastic doll category. Baby Lisa, introduced in 1980, is an 11-inch vinyl reproduction of an Astry Campbell porcelain doll in the permanent collection of the Smithsonian Institution. But the vinyl's fine features and elaborate wardrobe place it, too, within the grand tradition of fine dollmaking. *Photo: Effanbee, used by permission*

226. Zap guns of colorful polystyrene are a collecting specialty. The blue "Electra" has a tiny light at the tip. The red one is actually a Pez dispenser made in Austria. *Dennis J. O'Donnell*

ually changing lifestyle. She has been everything from a stewardess to an Olympic athlete to a student (however, there were no books on her campus). She is fully jointed and thus "poseable." One version can even pucker up to give a kiss. If children are the best judge of good toy design, Barbie is an unqualified success.

Although all Barbies are collectible, the first limited edition is most valuable, worth about $800 in mint condition. It has Cleopatra makeup and holes in the feet for attaching high heels. But also valuable is her kid sister, Growing Up Skipper, who got taller and grew breasts when her arm was cranked backward. The toy collector Ted Menten observed in a *Daily News* interview that this "hideous doll" was produced for only one year, and thus is rare, a factor that makes it—to some—desirable. Unlike Barbie, Skipper was not included in the Bicentennial time capsule.

Outside of the somewhat frenzied collecting mainstream are dolls of un-

adult collectors who belong to Barbie clubs and publish a Barbie newsletter, encyclopedia, and current price guide. Barbie's success surprised everyone in the doll industry, maddened feminists who called her sexist and materialistic, but it also provoked serious research on the part of one Yale art-history student, Ella King Torrey. Ms. Torrey devoted a year to Barbie research, concluding that "You can tell by the years, really, where the popular mind is in

America by just examining the various artifacts and accessories that are included in Barbie's dreamworld." Barbie, who initially had been rejected by the Sears catalog for being too sexy, eventually won that conservative emporium's approval. In 1980, her 21st birthday year, Sears devoted nearly three pages to Barbie, her considerable wardrobe, her friends (46), and her accessories. Barbie's appeal to children and adult collectors is her contin-

usual design and often remarkable beauty that are promoted—sometimes, briefly—and then are removed from the market if they do not continue to sell a certain volume. In this category are two anatomically correct male baby dolls, Baby Tender Love and Joey Stivic, the latter named for the baby on the TV show *All in the Family*. Although the manufacturers had market-tested the idea with favorable response from parents, the dolls were removed from the shelves after only about two years, in the late seventies, presumably because they did not sell. Such dolls are rare in the U.S. today, although not in Europe where they are common.

Dolls for boys, which the industry calls "action figures," have traditionally featured toy soldiers as the most popular category. Plastics largely replaced cast metal in the fifties for military miniatures, and in 1964 Hasbro Industries, Inc., introduced a foot-high single figure, "G.I. Joe." Bristling with weaponry, the figure sold well, around ten million a year, until about 1975 when antiwar sentiment cooled children's enthusiasm for militaristic toys. (One U.S. Army spokesman observed that the Vietnam war had "soured kids' attitudes on war.") At the same time, the oil crisis made such a large figure too expensive to produce at a reasonable price ($5.00). The toy was therefore retired until the Iranian hostage crisis revived kids' interest (some might say bloodlust) in war and hero figures. Marketed today as "Defender of Freedom," Joe has shrunk to about 3 inches tall and is only one of nine members of an elite antiterrorist force that includes a sexy redhaired female figure named "Scar-

228

227–228. The warrior Daltanias, a contemporary toy from Japan's Godaikin Collection of ten super-robots, retains traditional samurai elements such as helmet and leonine breastplate. Made of plastic and die-cast metal, it (opposite) disassembles into three smaller robots: Velarios, the gold-legged lion; Gunper, a space vehicle; and Atlaus, a smaller warrior. Characters are based on animated television heroes popular in Japan. *Forbidden Planet*

let," whose specialty is the crossbow. Also part of the set are three bad guys from "Cobra Command" who want to "conquer the world."

Some of the most ingeniously designed plastics are battery-energized superheroes such as Superman and monsters like Godzilla, all avidly collected by children today. Also intriguing are the tiny windup plastics produced by novelty manufacturers in Japan and Hong Kong. Often delight-

fully silly, these miniatures are favorites of many adult collectors who look for the silliest possible examples, such as a bespectacled mouse frying an egg, a robotic pop-up toaster, or surrealistic red crabs that perform a hula-ish sideways dance.

It seems incredible that objects produced only a few decades ago in unprecedented numbers could possibly be scarce, and yet, because of the nature of plastics—their perceived

cheapness—and the fact that toys are often literally worn out by use, plastic toys from the past are not that easy to find. Plastic collectors can take some consolation in the fact that plastics as yet hold little sway within the context of traditional toy collecting, where cast iron, tin, wood, paper, and cloth are most valued. Therefore, plastics are not in competition with the well-organized toy collecting establishment.

Among the rarest plastics are the

229

229–230. Capsela, a motorized construction set introduced by Play-Jour, Inc., in 1983, offers an ingenious system of interlocking gears and polycarbonate plastic capsules, each of which performs a special function. There are, for example, motor, speed reduction, rotary switch, and transmission capsules that can be used to build hundreds of working models that incorporate principles of physics, electricity, flotation, and aerodynamics. Sets are varied as to complexity and number of pieces and include the "Space Link" variation, opposite. The space station module has a work center for communication and navigation, a laboratory for computer control. Capsules form many types of spacecraft and robotic devices. Capsela is in the Design Study Collection of the Museum of Modern Art, New York. *Photos: Play-Jour, Inc.*

early molded Bakelite (phenolic) toys, such as the miniature Austrian car on page 150, the cast phenolic resin baby toys (page 149), and streamlined plastics in general. Plastics from the fifties and sixties are more abundant, with the most popular forms being vehicles and early space toys such as zap guns and robots. Space toys are a rich area for contemporary collecting. The Japanese have continued, since the Occupation, to be among the foremost designers

and producers of toy robots. They have, like the rest of the world, shifted heavily to plastic and die-cast metal combinations. Many of their toys are tied to animated television series, so models change as characters are created and written in and out of the shows. There is, therefore, a constantly changing cast of space characters of remarkable variety, among them the Daikin collection illustrated on page 162. Robots can be very expensive, up to $70 or more,

230

depending on the complexity of the toy. The Daikin warriors, for example, can be broken down and reassembled into smaller characters.

Whether you are collecting toys from the past or the present, your choices probably will be influenced more by your childhood preferences than by modern criteria of so-called good product design. Toys resist such classification. They are, as designer Charles Eames remarked, "less self-conscious than any other design form." Frequently, the fact that a toy is flimsy and ephemeral adds to its appeal. A child presented with a beautifully carved wooden airplane that represents a high degree of craftsmanship may in fact prefer a cheap, very realistic plastic plane that is closer to what he or she recognizes as the real thing. Adult toy collectors tend to react the same way, preferring the artifacts of their own childhoods to what currently may be considered worthwhile, "educational," or "well made." There is, for example, well-publicized adult antipathy toward sexist toys and violence toys—guns, war machinery, etc.—and in some countries, notably Scandinavia, such toys are not sold at all. Yet the enthusiasm for collecting dolls and toy soldiers remains high among both children and adults. In this regard there is no difference between traditional and plastic-toy collecting.

5 COMFORTS OF HOME

"Bakelite table tops withstand the years, the drinks, the cigarettes."

Bakelite Information, 1931

FACING PAGE:
231. A biomorphic fiberglass desk was created in 1969 by the sculptor Maurice Calka, winner of the Grand Prix de Rome, for the French firm Leleu-Deshay. As this prototype shows, it was designed to be fitted with electronic circuits for telephone, intercom, and television monitor. The adjustable swivel chair is fastened to the integrally molded, swooping right arm. (The aluminum lamp was designed in 1972 by Lebovici.) *Photo: Christie's, New York*

Furniture

Plastic materials appealed to the Modernist designers of the late twenties and thirties on many levels. Plastics were congenial with the democratic tenets of modernism that, among other things, promoted the use of industrial materials and mass-production. But plastics were also stylish, practical, and adaptable to different techniques of application, depending upon the form in which the materials were used. Plastic materials provided the first synthetic finishes in the form of cellulosic lacquers, and the first surfacing laminates, such as Formica, both of which came into wide use in the thirties. In the postwar era, acrylics, reinforced plastics (fiberglass), molded thermoplastics, and rigid and resilient foams largely revolutionized the technology of commercial furniture-making.

Celluloid, the first forming plastic, was rarely used in furniture and accessories. However, in the twenties and early thirties, designers sometimes used it to simulate ivory inlay, a favored technique among Art Deco cabinet-makers. One can find, for example, chests grain-painted to resemble exotic woods and trimmed in thin strips of ivorylike Celluloid. In 1922, the noted designer Eileen Gray used sheets of smoked Celluloid and chrome to create a decorative screen. Said to be the first use of Celluloid in furniture design, the piece sold at auction in 1980 for $21,950. Celluloid was also occasionally used to create low-wattage lamps, but examples are rare.

Synthetic Lacquer

Much more significant was the development in 1925 of nitrocellulose lacquer, a considerably diluted formula of the basic ingredients from which Celluloid was made. As a quick drying high-gloss finish, synthetic lacquer afforded Modernist designers a tough moisture-resistant finish with the look of natural lacquer (see Glossary). It was, however, infinitely easier to apply. Black-lacquered wood surfaces were usually teamed with tubular steel or aluminum in the creation of tables, desks, and cabinets in the Functionalist style. In

232

DESKEY

the early thirties, the innovative artist/ designer Donald Deskey experimented with synthetic lacquers to create magnificent ornamental screens. Factory-made furniture was often sprayed with lacquer, as were automobiles rolling off the assembly line at the Ford plant in Detroit. While natural lacquer dried very slowly, the synthetic version dried quickly through the evaporation of a volatile solvent upon contact to air. This desirable quality speeded up production of both decorative and utilitarian objects. While cellulosic lacquers are still in use for specialized applications, the gleaming finishes of much contemporary "lacquered" furniture is achieved by means of polyurethane and polyester resin coatings. These are tougher and harder than cellulosics. In some cases, such as the desk designed by Brian Kane on page 205, a thick layer of polyester resin is actually cast on a base material so that the surface and finish become, in effect, one and the same.

Laminate

But it was the development of surfacing laminates such as Formica that represents the first genuine structural application of plastics in furniture design. The laminated surface, unlike the lacquered surface, is actually a solid sheet about 1/16 of an inch thick. It is created by impregnating with phenolic resin several layers of material, usually an unrefined paper called kraft paper, then compressing (or laminating) the sheets under heat and pressure between plates of polished steel. The resultant single sheet may appear dull or glossy depending upon the degree

234

233

232. Donald Deskey's unique three-paneled screen, entitled "Lysistrata," was created with cellulosic lacquers about 1930 for the drama critic Gilbert Seldes. *Photo: Christie's, New York*

233. Deskey used metal and plastic laminate to create much of the furniture for Radio City Music Hall in 1933. Both tables shown here, and floor lamp, exemplify his stylish adaptations of Bauhaus designs for the theater that became one of the world's great Art Deco monuments. *Photo: Radio City Music Hall Archives*

234. Marcel Breuer's "Laccio" table, designed at the Bauhaus in 1925, pioneered the use of polished tubular steel in furniture design. Originally it had a top of lacquered wood, but this modern version produced by Knoll since 1960 has a plastic laminate top. *Photo: Knoll*

235

236

235. Donald Deskey designed this table in the early 1930s with an adjustable-height aluminum base so that it could function either for coffee or card-playing. The 28-inch-square top is surfaced with black plastic laminate. It sold at auction in 1982 for $1,210. *Photo: Hollander Gallery, Ltd.*

236. A small end table like this with a black laminate top and U-shaped chrome steel base is a Moderne popularization of the right-angled Bauhaus style. *50:Fifty*

237. This Bakelite and metal gaming table came from the Cafe Kipe in France in the 1930s. *Photo: Galerie Roudillon; Christian Gervais*

of polish on the steel plates. It is applied to a solid surface (wood, plywood, or chipboard) with special adhesives. Any decorative pattern is achieved by means of the photolithographic process. A laminate is a wholly industrial material, the antithesis of handcraftsmanship, and as such was ideally suited to the Functionalist style. However, the original Breuer and Breuer-type furniture did not incorporate laminates as far as we know. It was not until the early thirties that laminates for decorative purposes became widely available to interior designers.

Dr. Leo Baekeland, inventor of the phenolic resin Bakelite, obtained the first laminating patent in 1911. But he subsequently worked with two young engineers at the Westinghouse Corporation—Harold A. Faber and Daniel J. O'Connor—in the development of a paper-based laminate intended for use as electrical insulation. Their formula resulted in the establishment of the Formica Corporation in 1913. The company was so named because the new product was a substitute "for mica," a mineral that until then had been the most common electrical insulation material.

According to Formica corporate history, it was not until the mid-1920s that laminate was produced for the furniture industry. Until about 1925, all laminate was black or dark brown; but in 1927 Formica patented a method for producing decorative effects by means of a top layer printed as a lithographed sheet on a flatbed press. The earliest patterns imitated wood-grains and marble and were instantly popular in restaurants, bars, and soda fountains. But

throughout the thirties, the glossy black laminates remained the preference of sophisticated designers working in the Modern style. In America, for example, Donald Deskey combined black laminate with chrome-plated steel and aluminum in his designs for Radio City Music Hall. Some designers, however, judged wood-grain laminates perfectly suitable for such prestigious applications as the Library of Congress and the luxury liner *Queen Mary*.

Since 1937, the topmost decorative layer of most laminates has been impregnated with melamine. Not only does melamine impart increased surface hardness and water resistance, it facilitates the production of light colors. The reason for this is that melamine resin is colorless and does not alter the hue of coloring agents. Phenolic resin, however, is a dark amber color in its natural state and is not congenial with light tones. This is why most laminate displays a dark edging line that was eliminated only in 1982 with Formica's state-of-the-art laminate Colorcore. Colorcore utilizes more highly refined paper and melamine resins exclusively in order to achieve a sheet that is permeated with color. As a result, when edges of Colorcore laminate meet, there is an almost invisible seam and the object appears solid.

The designers of patterns for laminates have been concerned almost exclusively with producing more and more convincing simulations of natural effects such as wood-grain and marble. While most patterns are still produced by means of photolithography, manufacturers have discovered ways to use glitter and metallic sheet and even to

237

"sculpt" surfaces to resemble stone-work. At one time, Formica produced Realwood, a laminate in which the surface layer is actually a thin sheet of wood veneer impregnated with melamine resin. In some cases, linen-look surfaces were created by impregnating 100 percent cotton fabric for the top layer—cotton being the only material that can withstand the pressure in processing without disintegrating.

In the fifties, laminate was being promoted heavily for use in every room in the home. Formica Corporation hired Raymond Loewy Associates to create a new upgraded color line that included patterns now classified as "atomic" or "biomorphic"—black and pastel boomerang shapes floating in a white field. Patterns, however, were used almost exclusively for kitchens while wood-grains and the like were deemed suitable for other rooms in the home, especially when teamed with wrought iron and bamboo. (In 1951, *Living for Young Homemakers* magazine declared that "durable, well-designed, easy-to-clean plastics are engineered for the young way of living. . . . Today's homes have no room for museum pieces.")

Given the unlimited graphic-design potential of laminates, it is surprising that that aspect of the material has been so conservatively explored until recently. The most striking use of patterned laminate to date has been by Memphis, an international design group based in Milan. In 1982, Memphis introduced a radical line of furniture whose forms derive, as the name implies, from imagery as diverse as rock and roll and ancient Egypt. These were provocative,

238. A Lucite bedroom suite designed for Helena Rubinstein by Landislas Medgyes in 1940 included an acrylic sleigh bed illuminated by fluorescent fixtures. Side chairs and tables, all with engraved rose monogram decoration, completed the set. Madame Rubinstein is said to have commissioned the ensemble after approving the Lucite packaging for her cosmetics. It sold at auction in 1966 and was later acquired by a private collector of Art Deco and American Empire antiques.

239. An acrylic étagère made in the 1940s holds a collection of perfume bottles on its glass shelves.

perplexing, and humorous concepts in which busily patterned and violently colored plastic laminate surfaces figured as an integral part of the design. Squiggles, stripes, chevrons, and solids in brilliant contrasting colors demonstrated the power of graphic art to transform beds, bookcases, tables, and even clocks and lamps into works of (Pop) art (pages 13; 202–203).

Acrylic

Acrylic resin was introduced in 1927 but was not widely used commercially until the forties. It provided designers with a material that brought the glamor of transparency and unique light-transmitting properties not only to furniture and lighting design but also to architectural applications such as ceiling panels and murals. Acrylic is usually cast as sheet, rod, or tube. As a thermoplastic, it is easily heat-formed to create curved surfaces. It is also easily cut, lathe-turned, and solvent welded or molded in complex shapes. Expen-

239

240

241

240. A formal silk-upholstered side chair designed by Lorin Jackson and manufactured by Grosveld House, New York, in the early 1940s has legs and molded swag-and-tassel back ornament of acrylic. *Photo: Sotheby Parke-Bernet/EPA*

241. A boudoir stool with acrylic base and zebra-print original seat fabric is a good example of modernistic design from the early 1940s. *Maison Gerard*

242. Pioneering plastics artist Domenico Mortellito designed this lounge chair in 1940 using cast sheets and rods of Lucite for the base and post-formed sheets for the arms. The seat was covered with a leather-look plastic. *Photo: Domenico Mortellito*

sive tooling is generally not necessary. The glamor of acrylic, its ease of forming and versatility appealed both to high-style designers and more restrained modernists.

Acrylic furniture made before World War II is relatively rare; but the examples that do exist include bizarre as well as elegant pieces. Sometimes, both features are found combined, as in the side chair with molded acrylic tassels and upholstered silk seat on this page. That type of chair, with its allusions to period styles, provoked a diatribe in 1945 from the British industrial design historian John Gloag: "I have seen some experimental types of furniture made from various plastics, which disclosed the absence of a designer or the laziness of a designer, if indeed one was employed. In some examples, chairs of traditional form had been made in a transparent plastic, so that shimmering ghosts of Queen Anne or Chippendale models had unhappily materialised; in others, chair frames were constructed from transparent rod, bound together in imitation of the technique used for constructing cane furniture. An air of slightly uneasy luxury was conferred upon these articles, because transparent materials possess a luxurious quality, but they were destitute of original inspiration in design; true, they were unusual, but only in the way that Cinderella's glass slipper was unusual. Such things could only be produced by people who were still in the 'substitute' stage of thinking about plastics."

Gloag's attack contrasted with views of interior decorating magazines of the forties in which such designs might be characterized as possessing "suave

242

243

243. Gilbert Rohde designed this glass-topped occasional table with demountable Plexiglas tubes for legs in the 1930s. Solid brass bushings are threaded to the tubes at both ends, and the leg is attached to the glass top by a solid brass screw. *Photo: Rohde Family Collection*

244. An early example of the use of acrylic and glass for table design is by Eugene Schoen, a leading American designer of the 1930s. Manufactured for Schmieg-Hungate and Kotzean around 1934, it has a 36 inch-long glass top and 20 inch-high acrylic supports joined by a brushed aluminum stretcher. *Photo: Sotheby Parke-Bernet/EPA*

Plywood

Phenolic resin also vastly improved the process and technique for the manufacture of plywood, another type of laminate. Since its invention in the mid-19th century, plywood had been more akin to veneering, a process in which a thin sheet of decorative wood is applied to a solid core, usually of a cheaper wood. In the creation of plywood, where irreversible bonding is desired, the traditional adhesives such as animal-hide and casein glues never had been entirely satisfactory. They did not effectively resist moisture and were highly susceptible to warping, cracking, and vermin infestation. Phenolic resin eliminated these problems while contributing phenomenally increased strength and flexibility. The resin made it possible to compress multiple thin layers of wood into large sheets. By arranging the grain of alternate layers to run at right angles to each other, the ply sheet acquired great strength. It also could be bent or formed in graceful curves before the resin cured. In bentwood furniture, introduced by Thonet in the mid-19th century, this was achievable only with certain solid woods that were softened by steam and dried in steel forms. Resin-bonded plywood made the artful furniture designs of Charles Eames and the Finnish architect Alvar Aalto achievable in the fifties. Although this type of furniture is plastic only in the broadest sense of the term, its beauty is a by-product of plastic materials.

245. George Nelson's comfortable secretarial chair with articulated cradle back and swag seat of molded FRP was introduced by Herman Miller in 1958 and produced for only one year. *Photo: George Nelson Associates*

246. The Eames ETR table, nicknamed the "surfboard," was introduced by Herman Miller in 1951 but produced only until 1965. The wire base, similar to Eames's chair bases from the 1950s, supports a plastic laminate top 7½ feet long. Originally priced at $53.00, it sold at auction in 1982 for $1,500. *Photo: Charles Eames; Herman Miller Company*

247-248. Plastic shell chairs designed by Charles Eames can be dated to the 1950s by the now-obsolete wire-strut bases nicknamed "Eiffel Tower" and "cat's cradle." The rocking armchair, no longer produced commercially, is available only to Herman Miller-employed mothers-to-be. *Photos: Herman Miller Company*

245

246

247

248

249

249. Saarinen's pedestal collection was introduced by Knoll in 1956. It includes a table, with either plastic laminate or marble top, and the tulip chair, with a shell of molded FRP on a cast-aluminum base with fused plastic finish. The pedestal bases were conceived to eliminate what the designer viewed as the "slum of legs" that made typical interiors "ugly, confusing and unrestful." This interior is typical of the open-plan style of the 1950s. *Photo: Knoll*

elegance." One of the most famous examples of acrylic "period" design is the bedroom suite designed for Helena Rubinstein by Landislas Medgyes, probably in the early forties (page 172). Mme. Rubinstein supposedly commissioned the suite after viewing designs for her Lucite cosmetic containers. In his biography of her, *Madame*, Patrick O'Higgins describes his first vision of Mme. Rubinstein esconced in the illuminated sleigh bed:

'"Entrez!" Madame Rubinstein's voice resounded in French as I fiddled with the knob.

I stepped into her bedroom. It was huge, at least thirty feet long, and freezing. . . .

I now focused on Madame Rubinstein. She was reclining in state, at the far end of the room on what appeared to be a crystal sleigh.

"Come in! Come in!" she summoned me impatiently with both her hands.

250

She had the look of a Chinese doll—
tightly encased in a red quilted bed
jacket, black hair streaming over her
shoulders, while masses of pillows
propped her up.

"You're late! Sit down. . . ." She
pointed to one of several high-backed
chairs made of the same transparent
materials as her bed. The sun's reflec-
tions seemed to illuminate Madame and
her bed with subtle, incandescent light.
Then I realized, with a start, that the

curved head and foot boards were actually lit by fluorescent bulbs.

I must have nervously examined the
chair Madame pointed to, wondering
if it would hold my weight, because,
as if reading my thought, she said:
"Perfectly safe! Lucite! Same stuff as
our powder boxes.'' '

The theatrical notion of an illuminated
acrylic bed was a fleeting phenomenon if one is to judge by the several

250. A dining table designed by Vladimir Kagan in
1952 and manufactured by Kagan-Dreyfuss, Inc.,
utilized Formica's Realwood, a laminate surfaced
with a thin sheet of wood veneer impregnated with
melamine resin. Imitation wood laminate is produced by means of photolithography. *Photo: Vladimir
Kagan, Inc.*

251. Eero Saarinen's "womb" chair, designed for Knoll, utilizes a fiberglass-reinforced shell upholstered with foam rubber and fabric. The commodious form was Saarinen's response to Florence Knoll's request for "a great big chair you can curl up in." It has been in production by Knoll since 1956. *Photo: Knoll*

252. The "Kaleidoscope" armchair of acrylic sheet with metal fittings and leather cushion was designed by Jacques Famery in 1968 and manufactured by Polytechnique du Siege, Noisy le Grand, France. *Photo: Ferdinand Boesch, from "Plastic as Plastic," American Craft Museum of the American Craft Council, 1968-69*

253. The "egg" chair, a modern classic designed in 1957 by Danish architect Arne Jacobsen, owes its sculptural form to an inner shell of molded, rigid polyurethane foam. *Photo: Danish Information Office*

251

examples illustrated in *Interior Design* magazine in 1940; one designed by Paul Bry, another by R. D. Harrell. In the same year, Dave Swedlow, today a major producer of acrylics for the aircraft industry, as well as a line of high-style acrylic furniture, indulged a flight of fancy in the creation of an acrylic dining table. It included a bubbling fountain beneath the transparent surface and a photoelectric cell that activated a music box—all so that diners could enjoy the mingled sound of rippling water and romantic melodies. Another designer, William Zaiser, mounted a wooden grand piano on an S-curved Plexiglas base one-inch thick, four-feet wide, and over five-feet long.

Domenico Mortellito, an artist who created the Lucite mural for Du Pont at the 1939 World's Fair, made chairs, tables, cabinets, and sculpture of Lucite, each a unique experimental piece, to furnish his New York apartment in 1940. He recalled that, although visitors loved it, few manufacturers were

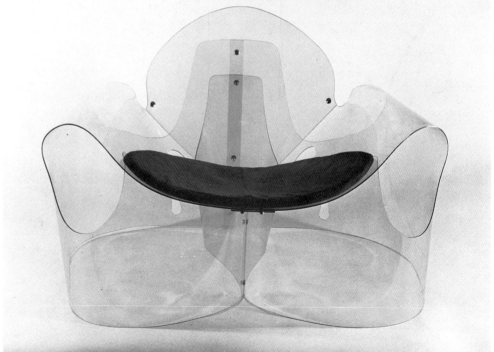

252

253

willing to produce acrylic furniture then because they knew too little about its properties. In fact, dealers report that early acrylics often display stress marks and crazing.

Of the designers in the mainstream of the modern movement, Gilbert Rohde was one of those most enthusiastic and innovative in the incorporation of plastics in furniture design. Like many American designers, Rohde produced tubular steel (or aluminum) furniture with laminated surfaces, his for the Troy Sunshade Company. He was also one of the first to use vinyl as an upholstery fabric and to combine acrylic with glass in the creation of occasional tables and for handles and legs on the wooden furniture he designed for the Herman Miller Company in the thirties. Rohde was also among the first to attempt a chair shell of plastic. His design had a stainless steel frame supporting a continuous sheet of acrylic curved to conform to the body. The *Christian Science Monitor* called it "most adventurous" in 1939, as indeed it was.

Acrylic did not truly come into its own for furniture until after the war when forming techniques were better understood. And not until the late sixties and early seventies did the design begin to lose some of the fussy conventionality it acquired during the fifties—often under the name of "ethereal delicacy," as design writers were wont to enthuse. The popularity of minimalist interiors helped turn designers toward simpler, more sculptural forms. In 1967, for example, *Domus* magazine featured an all-white minimalist room designed by the architect Leonardo Fiori in which light was considered a formal factor of

254

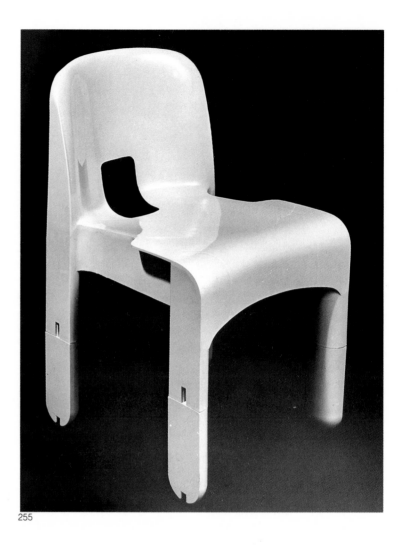

255

254. Verner Panton's cantilevered chair was the first to be made in one piece and entirely of plastic, including the base. Designed by the Danish architect in 1960, it was first manufactured of fiberglass-reinforced polyester by Herman Miller AG of Basel, Switzerland, and then by the same firm in America from 1973 to 1975. It nests for storage. *Photo: Herman Miller Company*

255. The "Seggio" stacking chair designed by Joe Colombo for Kartell in 1967 was the first to be formed by injection-molding. Although early examples were made of ABS, it is now produced in less-expensive polypropylene. *Photo: Ferdinand Boesch, from "Plastic as Plastic," American Craft Museum of the American Craft Council, 1968-69; courtesy Hank Loewenstein*

design, "even in the furniture, all of which is made of transparent acrylic which polarizes the light and makes it appear luminous along the edges . . . accentuating their outlines and forms."

An American designer noted for his innovative and stylish use of acrylic is Vladimir Kagan. Kagan's well-known sculptural techniques with wooden furniture were extended to acrylic, which he used as bases for luxurious upholstered pieces and in combination with

rare woods, as in the crescent desk he designed in 1976. Like other contemporary designers such as Dave Swedlow, Kagan displays a tendency toward the use of more massive pieces that allow the optical properties of the materials full play.

Reinforced Plastics

The development of reinforced plastics during the war held great significance for the furniture industry. The Navy had

256

257

been the first to experiment with impregnating natural fibers such as sisal, then glass fibers, with polyester resin to create a reinforced plastic that could be formed in low-cost, low-pressure molds. Polyester resin, derived from petrochemicals, was a thermoset that would polymerize in the presence of a catalyst and without the application of heat and high pressure. This characteristic made it ideal for shaping large, extremely strong forms such as radar domes and boat hulls without expensive compression molds. The FRP (fiberglass reinforced plastic) process basically involved laying the reinforcing fiber in an open mold by hand, spraying it with resin, usually by hand, and allowing it a few minutes to cure. After the war, FRP came into wide use in the civilian pleasure boat industry. The technology was already available (though not tailored to the furniture industry) when the young American architect

256. A cantilevered chair formed from a single sheet of acrylic was purchased in France in the 1950s and is from a set of four. *William Webber Gallery*

257. A polypropylene armchair for indoor or outdoor use was designed by John Yellen for Thonet in 1982. It is made in one piece by means of rotational molding, a process in which the mold itself is rotated about two perpendicular axes simultaneously. The system assures uniform wall thickness and strong corners. *Photo: Thonet*

259

FACING PAGE:
258. Finnish designer Eero Aarnio received the American Institute of Interior Designers award in 1968 for his FRP chair called "Pastille" in Finland and "Gyro" in America. It is suited to indoor or outdoor use, as a floating pool chair, for example, or even a sled. *Photo: Stendig*

259. Aarnio's "Ball," or "Globe," chair was first produced in 1966 by Asko of Finland. The concept of a hard outer shell of fiberglass surrounding a softly padded interior appealed to designers of science-fiction movie sets, who often used it to symbolize a kind of personal inner-space capsule. *Photos: Stendig*

produced commercially by the Herman Miller Company of Zeeland, Michigan. In 1948, the Eames entered the International Competition for Low-Cost Furniture Design held at the Museum of Modern Art in New York. Their entry, which won second prize for seating, was made of stamped sheet metal but was produced in plastic a year later for Herman Miller by Zenith Plastics (now Century Plastics) in Venice, California. Zenith, well-known to the Eames, had been a producer of FRP radar domes during the war. In *The Design of Herman Miller*, Ralph Caplan recounts that the production of the first shell chairs, using FRP and matched steel dies on hydraulic presses, was plagued with problems "that ranged from the hazard created by glass particles flying in the air at the plant to the challenge of devising a technique for letting fibers show through the surface without roughness." Caplan adds that although these problems were eventually solved over a nine-month period, "each of the

Charles Eames, together with his wife Ray, was exploring methods and materials for mass-producing an inexpensive chair.

Eames and the architect Eero Saarinen had entered and won first prize in the Museum of Modern Art's Organic Design in Home Furnishings Competition in 1940 with a shell chair made of resin-bonded plywood. The prototype, which necessitated bonding the plywood to a metal shell, was un-suited to mass-production techniques. And although Eames and his design group continued to research the problems, the war intervened and delayed work on private projects. Instead, Eames produced several molded plywood designs for the military that included medical splints and stretchers. At the close of the war Charles and Ray Eames returned to the problems of furniture design, and in 1946 they had their first molded plywood chairs

260

eral of the earliest and most famous designs, now classics, were produced by two noted Danish architects: Arne Jacobsen and Verner Panton. Jacobsen's graceful Egg and Swan chairs were both produced in 1957. The shells were molded not from FRP but of a high-density rigid polyurethane foam, which like polyester was another new petrochemical plastic. Jacobsen's chair, like Eames's and Saarinen's, was mounted on a steel pedestal base. But in 1960 Verner Panton designed the first all-plastic chair in which the base was integral with the seating shell. In addition, the cantilevered form of the Panton shell gave it the added advantage of being nestable. And both had wide implications for the contract (office and institutional) furnishings industry that would emerge in the early seventies.

The Decade of Single-shot Sculpture

The development of new plastics and forming methods accelerated in the late sixties and early seventies, giving rise to an incredibly diverse production of plastic furniture design. Two significant innovations were molded polyurethane foam and the adaptation by Italian designers of the injection-molding process for furniture production.

One of the earliest uses for molded foam was in the automobile industry; but by the mid-seventies this production technique had revolutionized furniture manufacture. Designers discovered that they could build a mold that represented the general form of the object, a chair or a sofa, for example; then they could place a strengthening frame of

early shells was practically handcrafted and the entire surface of each shell gone over with an emery cloth." Eames set the finished shells on complex wire strut bases (page 176), but subsequent designs had a simpler rod leg construction.

Eero Saarinen's larger and more luxurious "womb" chair, designed for Knoll in 1950, was also formed of an FRP shell. It was produced by the Winner Manufacturing Company, a producer

of boat hulls. Saarinen's chair, upholstered in foam rubber and fabric, and Eames's chair, with its many variations, were the first plastic shell chairs to be mass-produced and successfully marketed. Both have remained in constant production.

The sculptural, "organic" look of these chairs, and the plastics technology by which they were made, impressed and inspired designers all over the world to attempt similar pieces. Sev-

wood or metal into the mold, which was then closed and foam inserted in liquid chemical form. The chemicals would completely cover the frame and set up inside the mold almost instantly as resilient foam, after which the entire piece was removed as an integral unit ready for the application of fabric upholstery. In a variation of this technique called self-skin polyurethane (familiar as dashboard covering), the inner surface of the mold could be treated to produce a leather-look "skin" tough enough to take wear without further upholstery. In either case, the system eliminated traditional upholstery techniques in which springs, webbing, and multiple layers of padding were fitted and applied by hand. Mold forms could be as simple as a cube, or as complex as the "Marilyn" sofa (page 192). Once the mold was created, however, all that was required was a single-shot of chemicals to produce the soft "sculpture."

Similarly, rigid furniture forms could be produced by injection-molding, although the tooling was different and much more costly. In 1967 Joe Columbo designed the first injection-molded four-legged stacking chair, which was produced by Kartell. The material used was ABS, a strong nonreinforced plastic whose three ingredients—acrylonitrile, butadiene, and styrene—each contribute specific desirable structural qualities such as high impact-resistance, flexibility, and structural strength. ABS has the added advantage of a high gloss on both front and back surfaces. FRP is glossy only on the front side; the back is dull and the glass fibers are evident. Also, FRP production is slow and labor-intensive in comparison to

261

injection-molding. Injection molding of furniture is recommended when the piece to be produced is fairly small—such as a side chair—and large production runs are planned. Volume production is needed to offset the high cost of the steel dies used in injection-molding. A single mold for a small chair, for example, can cost as much as $50,000. The use of injection-molding has been most significant in the contract furnishings industry where high-

260. The flaring form of Joe Colombo's fiberglass "Elda" shell chair pays homage to its ancestor, the wing chair. *Photo: Stendig*

261. "Armchair 300," a white FRP upholstered shell, was designed by Pierre Paulin and produced in Holland by Artifort from 1965 to 1967. *Photo: Christie's, New York*

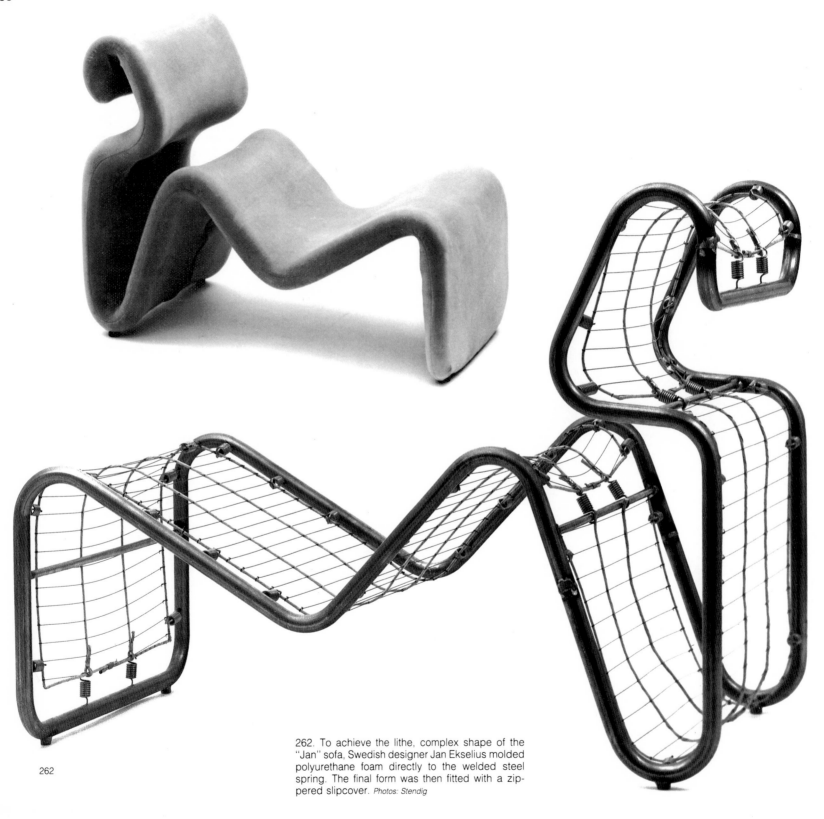

262. To achieve the lithe, complex shape of the "Jan" sofa, Swedish designer Jan Ekselius molded polyurethane foam directly to the welded steel spring. The final form was then fitted with a zippered slipcover. *Photos: Stendig*

262

volume light-weight stacking systems are called for. For this reason, most designers who in the fifties and sixties would have specified FRP now choose ABS, polyethylene, or other lightweight but strong thermoplastics. Eames chairs are among the few still produced in FRP, mainly out of respect for tradition.

Whatever process is used, the sculptural potential of the mold holds irresistible allure for designers. On the scale of furniture, the sculptural form, of course, assumes dramatic dimensions. During the seventies, fantasies were indulged to the hilt, but nowhere with more flamboyance and style than in Italy.

Modern Italian design evolved as Italy began to rebuild its devastated cities after the war. Concepts of industrialization in what had been essentially a nation of craftsmen gained impetus from American ideas of com-

263. The "Leonardo" chair, designed in 1977 by Paul Tuttle for heavy-use commercial areas, represents the first employment of self-skin molded foam in furniture design. *Photo: Atelier International, Ltd.*

264. An eccentric rocker by French designer Marc Held was produced briefly in the 1970s by Knoll in the United States. Held's design purported to "relieve the muscular contracture due to motionlessness" and accommodated the sitter's natural restlessness with a constant and simultaneous rock, swivel, and pivot on the convex FRP base. It had a brief production life. *Photo: Knoll*

263

264

265. "I Sassi" (The Rocks), a set of molded polyurethane boulders designed by Piero Gilardi in 1967, was manufactured in Italy by Gufram as a whimsical alternative to a chair. Small stones added a touch of realism to the grouping. *Photo: Stendig*

266–267. What appears to be a slab of engraved stone is actually a cocktail table of rigid, molded polyurethane foam. The Italian word "porfido" means porphyry, a type of igneous rock that was popular with sculptors of ancient Rome. Both "Porfido" and "Capitello," the molded foam lounge chair, at right, in the shape of a broken Ionic column, spoofed classical artifacts and materials by turning them into Pop objects. All were produced in Italy by Gufram in the mid-1970s. *Photos: Stendig*

268. The New York office of Alan J. Heller, president of Heller Designs, Inc., a leading producer of quality plastic housewares, is decorated largely with the company's products, as one might expect. These include stacking dinnerware and whimsical molded polyethylene lamps, among them Gladys Goose, the Barcelona Pear, and Snoopy. But Mr. Heller also collects Pop Art plastics from the 1960s that are incorporated into his office landscape. The *trompe l'oeil* "Handkerchief" table was designed by Studio Tetrarc of fiberglass-reinforced polyester. The "Cactus" hat rack by Guido Drocco and Franco Mello is made of molded polyurethane foam coated with waterproof paint. Both were produced in Italy by Gufram.

265

266

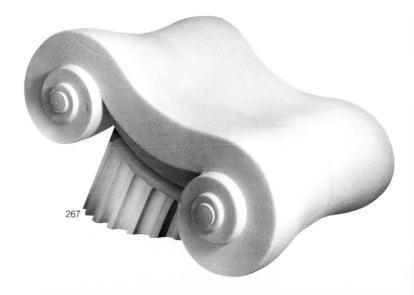

267

269

270

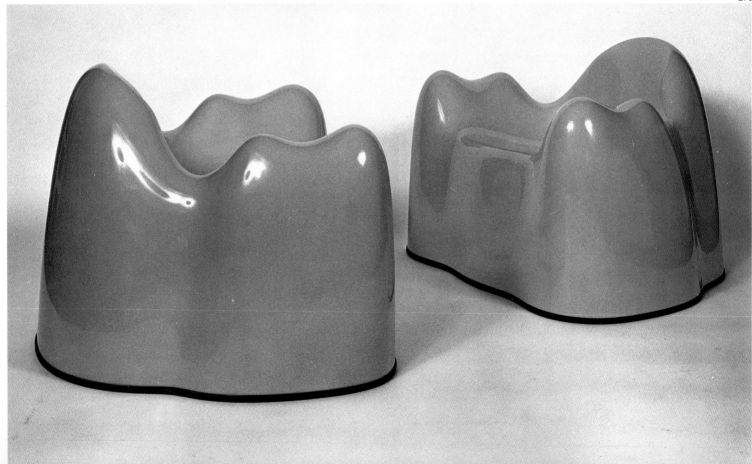

fort, leisure, and mechanization. In the 1950s, the architect Marco Zanuso began to emphasize the use of industrial methods, but on a small scale, an approach that proved congenial to the ingrained individualism of Italian craftsmen. The concept also met the real needs of the country in terms of increased production of goods and services. During the sixties, many small but prolific companies emerged, each of whose products in both furnishings and household objects displayed the stong style of its director, who was often the chief designer. Firms such as Cassina, Poltronova, Arflex (Studio Zanuso), Brionvega, Artemide, Gufram, and others were among the many whose goods were, by the early seventies, being imported into the United States. An elaborate and controversial exhibition of these products, titled *Italy: The New Domestic Landscape*, was presented at the Museum of Modern Art in New York in 1972. The 432-page catalog, today an essential reference for collectors of plastic and post-modern design in general, contained 520 illustrations and numerous essays relating to the development of Italian design in the 20th century. Just as the Bauhaus designs had expressed a social consciousness by proposing industrial materials and mass-production, Italian designers and theorists spoke of the need to develop designs that answered sociocultural problems and discouraged the "fetishism of goods" that they saw as "characteristic of our times." The need for more flexible living environments was addressed, for example, by designers who produced prototypical core living units of molded

271

269. The "Marilyn" loveseat was based on a surrealistic design by Salvador Dali. In 1937, Dali had conceived of Mae West's face as a room with her red lips forming a sofa. Jean Michel Frank created an upholstered version for Dali; but this one, designed by Studio 65 for Gufram in the 1960s, is formed of molded foam. It is usually produced with a lipstick-red nylon cover. *Photo: Stendig*

270–271. The American artist-craftsman Wendell Castle created a number of whimsical plastic furniture designs in the 1960s based on organic, abstract, and familiar forms. The armchair (opposite) from this "Molar" group is in the permanent collection of the Philadelphia Museum of Art. *Photos: Wendell Castle*

273

272. A polyester hippopotamus created by the French designer François Lalanne accommodates a bathtub in its body and a sink in its lower jaw. Fantasy furniture by Lalanne is in many private international collections. *Photo: Cosmos*

273. Eero Aarnio's "Mustangs" of molded polyurethane foam were renamed "Ponies" when sold in the U.S. by Stendig in the 1970s. A bit larger than a tricycle, they were nonetheless intended for commercial interiors, and a herd of them at one time inhabited the boardroom of a midwestern corporation. *Photo: Stendig*

plastic that could contain cooking, sleeping, living, and working space. Noble though these aspirations were, the most successful part of the exhibition was the display of alluring objects. In July, 1972, *Interiors* magazine described them as "not merely functional but elegant, endearing, visually refreshing and 'with it.'" In the same article, the architect Philip Johnson admitted that "this is the first major movement that makes Mies's Barcelona

chair look not exactly dated, but like what it is—a classic."

Among the plastic furnishings that looked only vaguely like what they were supposed to be were appealing Pop Art objects such as giant boulders, baseball gloves, and blades of grass presented as chairs, or, more precisely, things to sit on. Evidently, the intense and ascetic seriousness of modernism held little interest for the Italians, whose daring provoked designers in Europe,

Scandinavia, England, and the United States to attempt similar flights of fancy.

Among the many American importers of Italian (and Italian-inspired) design was Charles Stendig, whose firm, established in 1955, made a serious commitment to plastics in the sixties and seventies. The Stendig line included molded foam modules, upholstered conversation pits, and slick shell chairs, as well as humorous pieces. Even the company logo,

274, 275–276. Award-winning Italian designs from the 1960s that have continued in production by Kartell include Giotto Stoppino's nesting tables made of ABS plastic, and the child's stacking chair by Marco Zanuso and Richard Sapper of injection-molded polyethylene. Both were awarded the Compasso d'Oro and are in the design collection of the Museum of Modern Art in New York. *Black and white photo: Kartell; color photo: David Arky*

274

275

Stendig!, in those days occasionally sported an exclamation point as if to emphasize the vitality and exuberance of the product. In fact, Stendig was responsible not only for bringing many of the most memorable plastic designs to the United States but also for reviving classic modernist items such as bentwood chairs.

Most of the original Stendig plastic line is out of production. Notable exceptions include Eero Aarnio's "Gyro"

276

chair; the "Marilyn" sofa, enormous lips of molded urethane foam; and "Joe," the giant baseball glove of leather-upholstered foam. In a series of lectures on "The Evolving Chair," sponsored by the Cooper-Hewitt Museum in 1976, Stendig (who by then was no longer associated with the firm) commented that designs such as "Joe" and "Marilyn" were brought out "to give a little humor, a little color to the average commercial interior. . . . they are fun chairs, something we do not see very much of." Indeed, Stendig admitted that *Il Pratone* (literally "The Meadow," a mat of giant blades of polyurethane grass that he also imported) sold only about two in two years. This suggests that such pieces appealed more as artworks than as furniture—and that their not inconsequential cost required a buyer who not only could appreciate but also afford such an outrageous whimsy.

One of the least known but most appealing Pop designs is an enormous derby hat of fiberglass-reinforced plastic stuffed with a green foam-rubber apple to form a lounge chair. The design by Chilean artist Sebastian Matta was based on an idea by his friend the surrealist painter René Magritte. The chair, named MAgriTTA, has been produced in Italy by Simon International since 1970 as part of their Ultramobile line of surrealistic artist-designed furniture.

While Pop objects were ephemeral in nature, they were usually much more substantial in construction than the inflatable furniture presented in the late sixties as a practical solution to moving and storage problems of the urban nomad. The concept, like many other

277

277. Stacking storage units designed in 1970 by Anna Castelli Ferrieri are made of ABS plastic. With many variations and colors, this has become one of the most familiar of all modular plastic designs.
Photo: Kartell

278

278–281. In the early 1970s, the emerging contract furnishings industry demanded strong, lightweight, inexpensive seating systems for which plastics supplied an essential structural material. Numerous systems, such as "Nova," this page, designed in 1970 by Gerd Lange for Atelier International, Ltd., and Don Albinson's system for Knoll, opposite, utilize injection-molded plastic for seating elements. The engineering elegance of the systems is demonstrated dramatically when chairs are stacked for storage on a dolly. *Nova photos: Atelier International, Ltd.; Albinson photos: Knoll*

279

282. Mass, transparency, and luxurious texture combine in Vladimir Kagan's acrylic furniture designs from the late 1960s. Velvet-upholstered chair seats and glass table top appear suspended by the mere outline of form. *Photo: Vladimir Kagan, Inc.*

283. An informal and innovative interior from the late 1960s is furnished almost entirely with inflatable pieces, including sofa, armchairs, ottoman, and even lighting fixtures. *Photo: American Crafts Council*

284. A seating system designed in 1972 by Milanese architect Cini Boeri is luxurious yet adaptable to informal living spaces. Polystyrene seating frames fitted with leather-upholstered cushions are molded with open-shelf storage space in back. Wedge-shaped end tables permit sofa and settee to be angled toward each other. *Photo: Knoll*

285. "Environ One," manufactured in the 1960s by Niko Internazionale, Italy, for Stendig, consisted of eight basic molded foam seat and back units. *Photo: Stendig*

282

283

284

285

202

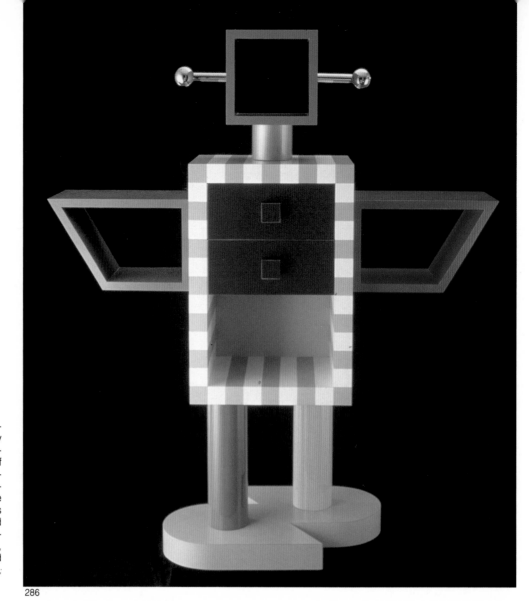

286

286–287. Brightly patterned surfaces of plastic laminate enliven the unusual furniture designs by Memphis. Manasori Uneda's "Ginza" robot storage shelf is more a presence than a piece of furniture, bearing—one would hope—friendly messages in its "chest of drawers." Opposite: "Casablanca," the huge dining-room sideboard of Ettore Sottsass, Jr., is aptly described by the designer as a "totem-credenza." Almost eight feet high, and completely covered with exotically patterned plastic laminate, it has storage drawers, cupboards, and slanted, outstretched arms meant to hold bottles. *Photo this page: Furniture of the Twentieth Century, N.Y.; Memphis, Milan*

space-age notions, appealed more in the abstract than in reality. (It was also not new. In *Plastics: Designs and Materials*, Sylvia Katz illustrates three pneumatic chairs designed in England in the forties, one by Elliot Equipment, a manufacturer of inflatable aircraft dinghies.) Inflatable chairs, such as "The Blow" by Scolari, Lomazzi, D'Urbino and DePas manufactured in Milan by Zanotta in 1967, had design cachet but were not comfortable. They gave the sitter a

bouncy, hence unstable, feeling and little support. Also, the vinyl skin, which did not "breathe," caused the sitter to sweat. Conservative furniture firms such as W. & J. Sloane in New York held these "novelties" in contempt and refused to stock them while scores of cheap knockoffs were used briefly and discarded. As a result, inflatables are probably among the rarest of all plastic furniture to be found today.

That any piece of plastic furniture

could be considered a rarity may soon cease to surprise those who automatically equate all plastics with cheapness and "mass-production." The term rightly describes many thousands of duplicates, but in fact many of the unusual and extreme postwar designs were produced in relatively low numbers. In addition, many of these same designs were sold exclusively through designer showrooms and could be ordered only through decorators and

287

architects. The scarcest designs are usually those made of fiberglass reinforced plastic. It was not unusual to manufacture only a few hundred a year, even of bestselling designs such as Eero Aarnio's "Gyro."

In December, 1983, at Christie's auction rooms in New York, several lots of plastic furniture less than twenty years old were offered in a sale of Important 20th Century Decorative Art. Included were designs by Pierre Paulin, Joe Colombo, Roger Tallon, Eero Aarnio, and the firm Leleu-Deshays. The Leleu desk that appears on page 166 was created in 1969 by the sculptor Maurice Calka at the request of the French firm. Described (by the donor) in the catalog as a fiberglass prototype, it sold for $11,000. Prototypes are regularly made by the FRP hand-lay-up method and differ hardly at all from the pieces that are finally put into production. Since the exact design was presented in both an article and an advertisement in the November, 1969, issue of *L'Oeil*, it may be safely assumed that there is more than one such desk in the world, but probably not many.

Lighting

In the modern house—Corbusier's "machine for living"—lighting and lighting fixtures were more often conceived of as a function of architecture rather than of ornament. By day window walls of glass (which translated in conventional terms to "picture windows") opened the modern home to natural light, while at night indirect lighting provided general diffused illumination that was considered healthier for the eyes than discrete pools of direct light from

adjustable, with, for example, articulated arms and counterweights by which the fixture could be raised or lowered.

Although plastics did not develop into an important lighting material until the 1960s, there were interesting early experiments with colored Celluloid, Bakelite, light-colored urea-formaldehyde plastics such as Beetle and Plaskon, and acrylic. While experiments with Celluloid are understandably rare due to the material's low heat resistance, Bakelite in combination with metal and glass became fairly common in the thirties in the creation of lamp bases (page 206) and even entire molded shades. A phenolic shade would be opaque and therefore provide only direct illumination, but molding offered the potential for striking formal design. The articulated Jumo lamp on page 209, produced in France in the forties, is one of the most dramatic examples of streamlining in any material. (The designer is unknown although dealers speculate that it may have been the Art Deco sculptor Gustav Miklos because of its resemblance to a work by him entitled "Locomotive.")

In 1940 or '41, Walter Dorwin Teague created an equally striking piece of streamlining with the redesign of a lamp for the Polaroid Corporation. Polaroid lamps incorporated a patented polarizing filter made of cellulosic film that eliminated glare. Their first lamp incorporating this feature was an unlikely boxy design (page 207) that produced only a dim crescent of work light. Teague's redesign raised the light source on a conical neck of brushed aluminum anchored to a molded Bake-

lamps. Ideally, indirect lighting fixtures were hidden from view, behind valances, within shelving, or in specially designed ceiling recesses. The resultant diffused light reduced the need for many small direct light sources, except those required for special tasks and close work. However, indirect area lighting was also accomplished with lamps. One of the most common Art Deco forms was the torchiere, usually an upturned shade on a slender column

that bounced light off the ceiling and back into the room. These were usually metal or glass in combination with metal.

Modern lighting fixtures from the twenties and thirties included, of course, the magnificent Art Deco glass lamps by Lalique, Daum, and other French masters. But these were created as works of art whereas Bauhaus-inspired designs of metal and glass were conceived in functional terms. Many were

289

lite base. It was the addition of a streamlined Bakelite shade, however, that not
only substantially increased illumination
but turned an otherwise peculiar object
into a remarkable piece of machine-
age sculpture. Around the same time,
Teague also designed a student lamp
for the Polaroid company that utilized a
copper-trimmed Bakelite base with a
clever elliptical shape that cast a long
beam of light across the desk. Inexpensive, it was conceived of as the mod-

ern successor to the gooseneck.

While desk lamps remained fairly
small in size, table lamps for formal living areas grew in height to accommodate the shorter end tables designed
for the new style of low-set, commodious, upholstered armchair. In the thirties and forties, modern lamp bases
might be tall chrome or glass cylinders,
while floor lamps might be aluminum
columns trimmed with black or brown
Bakelite in the manner of those de-

288. "Neapolitan," a table representing a block of
spumoni—the traditional Italian ice cream—was created by Lee Payne, IDSA, using Formica Corporation's innovative Colorcore laminate that is permeated with color throughout. This particular design
won second prize in Formica's 1982 "Surface and
Ornament" design competition that introduced
Colorcore to the market. *Photo: Formica Corporation*

289. A desk designed in 1983 by Brian Kane for
the Metropolitan Furniture Corporation has a ⅛ inch-
thick finish of cast polyester resin applied over a
structural core. The innovative aspect of the material is its ability to be repaired by means of sandpa-
per and ordinary furniture polish, which together
remove scratches, burns, and gouges. *Photo: Metropolitan Furniture Corporation*

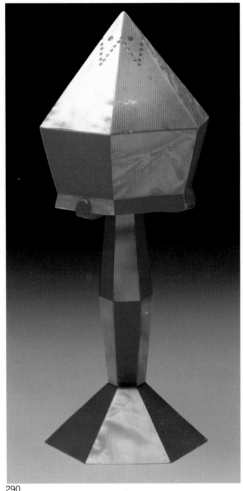

290

291

290. This ten-inch-high nightlight has a "Made in France" paper label on the base. Found in a midwestern antiques shop, it is probably Celluloid from the 1920s. *Douglas Taylor*

291. English globe lights and a French desk lamp by Jumo have molded Bakelite bases. *Photo: Galerie Roudillon, Christian Gervais*

signed by Donald Deskey for Radio City Music Hall (page 169). The ordinary consumer, long immersed in period furniture and lighting but with an urge to "go modern," was offered less severe styles that around 1940 might be made of acrylic. A typical acrylic lamp base from that period was a stack of cubes and balls surmounted by a fabric shade. Acrylic was also used in combination with glass and metals such as copper in chandeliers and sconces, and in one unusual case as fireplace ornaments shaped like acanthus leaves. They would, of course, melt if placed anywhere near a real fire. Although such designs could boast the use of a modern material, they were not so much modern as throwbacks to, and imitations of, the glass designs of earlier decades.

In 1948, the sculptor Isamu Noguchi (known later for his Akari paper lanterns) designed a small table lamp

292

293

constructed of a translucent plastic cylinder mounted on three slender, carved wooden supports. Simple, elegant, and inexpensive, the lamps inspired many imitators; by the sixties a raft of similar pure-form lamps were being produced in Europe, Scandinavia, and the U.S., not only in plastic but also in opalescent glass.

In a 1964 survey of contemporary lighting, *Industrial Design* magazine deplored the quality of the general run of so-called modern fixtures available in department stores, commenting on the "superabundance of Early American [reproductions] . . . Miami Beach baroque fixtures laden with cupids and rosebuds and bland Woolworth modern units. . . ." Of the noteworthy designs cited, most were simple geometric shapes in glass and metal, some in teak and sisal (materials popular with Scandinavian designers), but surprisingly few in plastic. The majority were

292–293. In 1940 the Polaroid Corporation designed this glare-free desk lamp with an odd boxy Bakelite housing. Judged an optical success but a design failure, it was redesigned the next year by Walter Dorwin Teague who gave it a brushed aluminum neck and streamlined shade (right). The result was modern sculpture with improved light range. *Left: William Greenspun; Right: 50:Fifty*

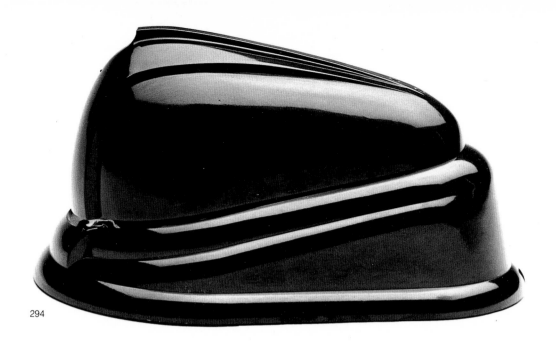

294

imported from Italy and Scandinavia. But if it appeared that American designers were lagging in good innovative design there was at least one notable exception who had set a new standard ten years earlier. In 1954, George Nelson enlisted plastic materials and wartime technology to create an inexpensive mass-produced hanging lantern. In an adaptation of a mothballing technique used by the military to rustproof stored equipment, he sprayed self-webbing vinyl over metal ribs (page 210) until the chemical formed a translucent spiderweb. A connecting ring secured the wires at top and bottom for rapid assembly without welding. Nelson was also one of the first designers to construct more complex and decorative lanterns from strips of extruded plastic film (page 210). Both of these designs and techniques have been widely imitated.

In the sixties and seventies, as modern lighting design became increasingly sculptural, ranging from organic to Pop, designers began to rely more on plastics. Italian designers were especially inventive with the materials, and many of the lamps by Gae Aulenti, Mario Bellini, the Castiglioni brothers, and Joe Colombo have become classics. These ranged from sleek multi-directional lamps formed of PVC pipe to elaborate acrylic light sculptures that were (not so simply) virtuoso performances with the material. Designers who worked with large complex shapes came to appreciate the light weight, strength, and diffusing characteristics of many types of plastics. Glossy ABS was strong yet lustrous, and resin-reinforced fiberglass was inherently beautiful when illuminated, allowing the glass fibers to appear as texture in the translucent sheet. Acrylic with its special edge-lighting characteristics and optical clarity remains the most elegant of all the plastic materials insofar as lighting is concerned.

Exciting forms, however, do not necessarily represent improved illumination. In 1983, Achille Castiglioni, a foremost contemporary lighting designer commented (in the catalog of the *Design Since 1945* exhibition) that, "In some of the most recent designs one finds that the interest is centered not so much on solving the problems of lighting in its fullest sense as on emphasizing the decorative quality of fixtures when they are without light." Indeed, in terms of improved light quality, the contribution of plastics is often hidden in the form of polarizing and diffusing filters, all the better to view the extravagant forms of 20th-century design.

Plastics in Interior Design

In the January, 1984, issue of *House & Garden* magazine, the editors published two dramatically different interiors. In the New York home of collector Barbara Jakobson, classic designs from the forties and fifties were assembled to recreate the ambience of those decades. Included with a Vladimir Kagan sofa and Noguchi table were fiberglass

294–295. The "Jumo" desk lamp is among the most sought-after streamlined artifacts. Made and patented in France in 1945, it combines a molded phenolic shade and base with an articulated chrome and brass arm. The shade can be angled in several directions and collapses into the base (detail). The "Jumo" was also made in green and in white casein plastic. *Maison Gerard*

295

low armchairs by Charles Eames and a vinyl upholstered armchair by Carlo Mollino. A few pages on, the home of noted American architects Robert Venturi and Denise Scott-Brown revealed an eclectic approach to design that effectively placed an orange molded plastic chair by Joe Colombo in a living room filled with Art Nouveau and Art Deco furniture. The collector whose bedroom is pictured on page 172 found it appropriate to mix acrylic pieces from the forties with fine American Empire pieces from the early 19th century. In her book *French Style*, Suzanne Slesin points to the use of the Jumo Brevette lamp (this page) as an art object in a Parisian living room. In each case, plastics make an evocative or provocative design statement. Their compelling machine-made forms, vivid colors, and the special qualities of the synthetic materials claim our attention as strongly as did the abstractions of Art Deco and the sensuousness of Art Nouveau in decades past.

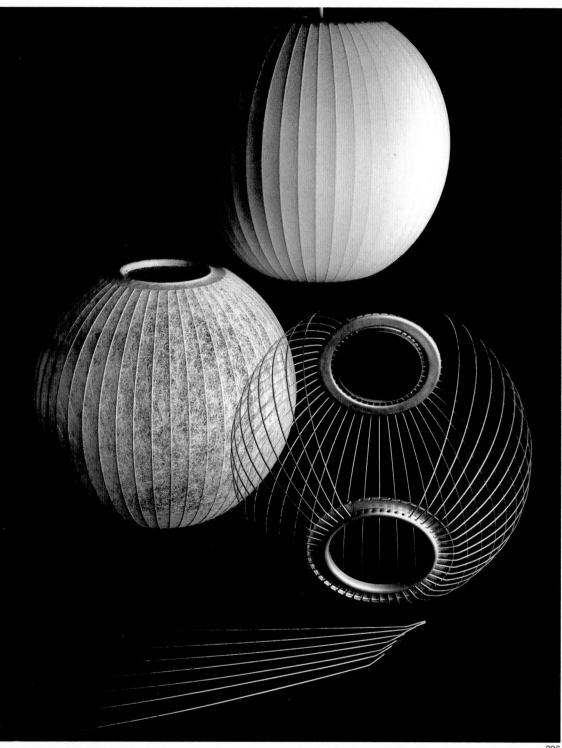

296

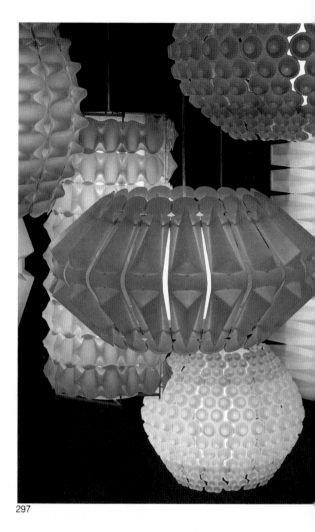

297

296–297. George Nelson's "Bubble" lanterns, designed in 1952 for Herman Miller, were created by spraying a cocoon of vinyl over metal ribs, an adaptation of a rustproofing technique used by the military. Nelson's decorative lanterns, designed in 1962, also for Miller, took advantage of the light weight and good diffusing properties of extruded plastic film. *Photos: George Nelson Associates*

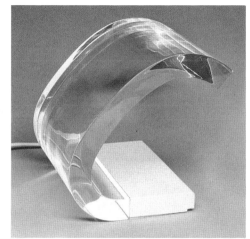

298.

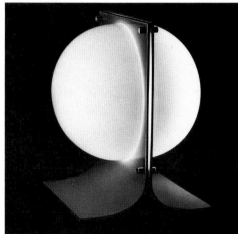

299.

298. The "Colombo" table lamp, designed by Joe Colombo in 1962, anchors an acrylic wave in a brass base where a small fluorescent bulb is housed. More effective as sculpture than illumination, it demonstrates the beauty of edge-lighting, an optical phenomenon peculiar to acrylic. *Photo: O-Luce*

299. A table lamp by Neal Small, 24 inches high and 20 inches wide, uses polished chrome hardware to join hemispheres of vacuum-formed acrylic. *Photo: Neal Small*

300. "Globo Tissurato," Ugo La Pietra's 28 inch-high lamp, is constructed of three acrylic hemispheres set into a cylinder. *Photo: Ferdinand Boesch from "Plastic as Plastic," American Craft Museum of the American Craft Council, 1968-69*

300

301

301. Vico Magistretti's "Snow" lamp, with shade of translucent acrylic, gives both diffused and directional illumination. *Photo: O-Luce*

302. The "Nesso" table lamp of molded ABS plastic was designed in 1962 by Gruppo Architetti Urbanisti Citta Nuova for Artemide. The mushroom form, 13¾ x 21⅝ inches in diameter, has become a modern classic. *Photo: Ferdinand Boesch, from "Plastic as Plastic," American Craft Museum of the American Craft Council, 1968–69*

303. "Bulb Bulb," a Pop Art lamp created in 1980 by the German designer Ingo Maurer assumes a color or not according to the type of 60 watt bulb used to illuminate the molded plastic one. *Photo: Ingo Maurer*

302

Acknowledgments

So many people helped in the preparation of this book that it would be impossible to name them all. The book could not have been done without the cooperation of the many collectors and dealers who lent objects for photography or of those who contributed photographs. Their names are noted at the end of each caption; however, in this last regard I am particularly grateful to Wendell Castle, Steve Diskin, Stanley Lechtzin, Bob Natalini, Ivy Ross, Michel Roudillon, and Neal Small. Thanks also to the many plastics industry professionals who helped me through the complexities of a difficult and unfamiliar subject: Wayne Pribble who read the manuscript for technical errors; J. Harry DuBois for guidance in the early stages of research; James Keegan (for research materials) and Dave George, both of Occidental Chemical Corporation; Kathleen Horning of Du Pont; Messrs. Plumpton, Landers, and Kilbury and Susan Lewin of Formica Corporation; Claire Ranere of Union Carbide; Ester Roche of Celanese Plastics Division; Jack Pounds of Rohm & Haas; Dennis Beck of Owens-Corning Fiberglas; Carolyn T. Stein of Mobay Chemical Corporation; Frank Saladino of Commercial Plastics; Mary Smith of Bakelite UK Ltd.; Frank Corbin of the Society of the Plastics Industry; and Andrew Connan. Among the museum, gallery, publishing, and library professionals who aided my research, I am grateful to Jean Drusedow and the staff of the Costume Institute, Metropolitan Museum of Art; David McFadden of the Cooper-Hewitt; Derek Ostergard; Rita Brand of Speakeasy; Lucien Goldschmidt for comments on plastic bookbindings that informed the paragraph on that subject; Chris Bailey of the American Clock and Watch Museum; Joann Polster of the American Craft Council Library; Stacey Crammes of the Hoover Historical Center; Carolyn Davis of the George Arendts Research Library, Syracuse University; Claire Silvers of MIT Press; George Barlow of the McGraw-Hill Library; and Robert Liu, editor, *Ornament* magazine. Thanks also to the designers and manufacturers who wrote of, or spoke with me about, their work in plastics: Jean Otis Reinecke for interesting letters on streamlined design; Donald Deskey for recollections about designs for Radio City Music Hall; Lee Rohde for access to the Gilbert Rohde scrapbooks; George Nelson Associates; Linda Folland and Linda Wagenveld of Herman Miller, Inc.; Elaine Caldwell and Irving Lepselter of Stendig, Inc.; Elinor McSweeney of Knoll; Phyllis McCullough of Thonet, Inc.; Elvin Chase of Metropolitan Furniture Corp.; Jill S. Coffey of Swedlow, Inc.; Jane Tourville of Atelier International; Lis King and Bob Perry of Kartell; Alan Heller of Heller Design; Richard Hochman of National Housewares Manufacturers Association; Jane Trimble of Tupperware; Deborah Van Woerkom of Howard Miller Clock Co.; and Barbara Radice of Memphis, Milan.

A special thanks to Sylvia Katz, Design Council, London, for her pioneering first book, *Plastics: Designs and Materials*, where I discovered the Barthes quotation on page 12, and for her new book *Classic Plastics*, which should prove a companion volume to this one; Medhat Abdel-Salam for the extended loan of essential reference works; Gerard Widdershoven for translating the Boymans catalog from Dutch into English; Shiuzo Imaizumi for help with photography sessions; Richard Giannadeo for printed materials; and Audre Proctor and Ted Panken for typing.

Deepest thanks to close friends for help above and beyond: Donna Carlson of the Art Dealers Association for generous continued assistance that included access to her vast and varied files; Linda Campbell Franklin for ideas, opinions, research materials, keen collector's viewpoint, and expertise, especially as concerns kitchen collectibles; and especially to Frank Farnham for patience, love, and support.

Finally, thanks to my editor Walton Rawls for allowing the book to grow and to David Arky for his beautiful and imaginative photographs.

Identifying Plastics

Few plastics can be specifically identified on sight; this is particularly true of the many complex synthetics developed since World War II. Identification is of concern primarily when questions of imitation materials arise in situations that bear directly on pricing. Objects made of natural substances such as amber, ivory, and tortoiseshell are generally priced higher than plastic imitations. Identification is also important when determining the best way to clean, care for, and/or restore an object.

Some plastic imitations are extremely convincing—particularly of amber (discussed below); however, a simple hot-pin test used by jewelers and amateurs alike can help to determine the precise nature of the material in question. The only equipment necessary is a long pin or needle and a heat source such as a gas flame. Electric hot-point testers are sold for this purpose by jewelers' supply firms such as the Gemological Institute of America.

Precautions

Basic precautions must be observed before and during the application of the hot-pin test:

(1) NEVER apply an open flame directly to any plastic—it may be cellulose nitrate, which will ignite instantly, thus destroying the object and possibly injuring the tester.

(2) Do not heat-test any extremely thin-walled object that you suspect to be Celluloid, such as the blow-molded objects on pages 14 and 19. Even a cold pin can pierce and hence mar such objects; a hot pin can cause serious damage.

(3) NEVER apply the hot-pin test to polyurethane foam, or any unidentified foamed plastics. Polyurethanes are highly flammable and emit an acrid smoke as they burn.

(4) Hold any object being tested away from the face as you apply the needle.

(5) Test in a well-ventilated space.

The Test

As noted in "The Nature of Plastic" on page 18, plastics are classified by how they respond to heat. But they also emit a characteristic odor when heated. Therefore the hot-pin test can both identify the material generally as either a thermoplastic or a thermoset, and more specifically as to chemical type (whether Celluloid, Bakelite, or acrylic, for example).

To apply the test, choose an inconspicuous spot such as the underside of a molding or the drill hole of a bead. In this way, you will not mar the surface. Heat the pin or needle in a flame until red hot, then touch the point to the object. If the object remains hard and rocklike, it is a thermoset such as phenolic molding. If it is easily penetrated, smokes, or strings like spun sugar, it is a thermoplastic such as Celluloid, acrylic, or polystyrene. Note the odor emitted when the pin touches the plastic and compare to the chart (page 216).

Natural Materials

Familiarity with natural materials is the best protection against being sold imitations. Real tortoiseshell, for example, has dark-brown irregular blotchy markings in contrast to the turbulent swirls seen in imitations. Ivory has irregular striations while those found on plastic imitations tend to be narrowly spaced and even. Pearlized plastics usually are apparent imitations, characterized by exaggerated crystalline patterns and found in frankly artificial tints of pink, green, yellow, and other pastels. Mother-of-pearl is gray or white with high iridescence. Synthetics simulate iridescence with a substance called *pearlessence* that is formulated from guanine (crystals obtained from fish scales) and mixed with synthetic resins. Artificial pearls, even the best quality, are usually shell or glass beads coated with multiple layers of *pearlessence*. In contrast, cultured pearls are formed in living oysters that coat an implanted shell bead with a natu-

HEAT TEST GUIDE

Material	Odor
NATURAL	
Amber	piney
Ivory	burned hair
Tortoiseshell	burned hair
Bone	burned hair
THERMOPLASTICS	
Acrylic	fruity
Cellulose nitrate	camphor
Cellulose acetate	vinegar
Nylon (molded)	burned wax or hair
Polycarbonate	weak phenol
Polyvinyl chloride	hydrochloric acid
Polyethelene	burned wax
Polystyrene	gas or marigolds
THERMOSETS	
Phenol-formaldehyde	acrid phenol
Urea-formaldehyde	formaldehyde
Melamine-formaldehyde	fishy
Polyester	sour cinnamon
Casein	burned milk
OTHER	
Polybern	sour cinnamon
Slocum	fruity

ral secretion called nacre. Semiprecious stone imitations are relatively easy to detect by eye and touch. Stone (and glass) is heavier than plastics and cold to the touch while plastics are relatively light and warm.

Amber and Copal

The most problematic imitations are those of amber, which are so widespread and convincing that they cause continual contention between collectors and dealers. Amber imitations were common before 1920. Caseins and cellulosic and phenolic resins were all used to create amberlike ornaments. Amber, a fossilized tree resin, has many of the same properties as plastics. Before the invention of plastics, amber could be identified by its electromagnetic properties—its ability to attract lint, bits of paper, and dust due to a buildup of negative electromagnetic charges. But plastics, also electromagnetic, made that test irrelevant. Amber expert and collector Dr. Patty D. Rice devotes an entire chapter to amber imitations in her authoritative book *Amber: Golden Gem of the Ages*. She discusses eight common imitations including Celluloid, phenolic resin, casein, polystyrene, acrylic, and the little-known lookalikes Slocum, bernit, and polybern (see glossary). True amber is soft and light enough to float in salt water. It ranges in color from honey tones to cognac-browns and reds. Nuggets usually contain internal fractures and bubbles formed over the centuries as water evaporated and as entrapped organic material exuded oxygen. When supposed old amber necklaces of faceted or smooth beads prove to be clear of these imperfections when examined under a magnifying glass, they should be hot-point tested. Because amber is soft, the facets and drill holes of old beads often show wear while plastic imitations stay sharp. Copal, a semi-fossilized amber-type resin, is also easily copied in plastics. It is usually encountered as opaque honey-colored or brown beads that often display surface crazing. Much of the ethnic jewelry from the Middle East, India, Nepal, and Africa contains real as well as imitation copal. According to Dr. Rice, much imitation copal now originates in Europe, where it is cast in broomstick-shaped moldings. These are sold to African craftsmen who cut the sticks into beads and sell them as "African amber" or "Somali amber."

The hot-point test for ambers and copals may be supplemented with additional tests such as the refractive index and specific gravity index, both of which are described by Dr. Rice.

Care and Cleaning of Plastics

Contrary to popular belief, plastics are not indestructible. They can crack, shatter, fade from constant exposure to light, and scorch. Thermoplastics scratch easily and are stained by alcohol and many types of chemical solvents. Most of this type of damage is permanent.

Dirt and grime may be removed with a luke-warm solution of soap and water and a soft cloth; never use abrasives. Very hot water and strong detergents may remove gloss; therefore plastics should not be put in the dishwasher unless marked as dishwasher-safe. Alcohol and acetone should not be used as cleaners, but turpentine, an oil, is an effective and nondestructive solvent for some types of dirt such as price-tag adhesive. There are several good plastic polishes on the market, some specifically for acrylic. One good all-purpose cleaner recommended by collectors is Novus II, available in specialized plastic stores.

Plastics Restoration

Because serious damage to plastics—cracks, burns, etc.—is irreparable, restoration is often limited to simple replacement of parts, such as radio knobs, and to surface cleaning. Upholstered elements on molded shell furniture sometimes can be replaced if they are not bonded directly to the molded surface. Pieces formed of molded foam over a structural frame pose major problems that may be insoluble without the cooperation of the original maker. Even so, the cost of re-molding may be prohibitive. More likely, the process may be impossible to recreate if the molds cannot be located.

Chipped laminates cannot be patched or filled, but entire laminated elements, such as table tops, can be replaced with relatively little trouble. This can be advisable if the base is tubular steel and easily detached from the top. In the case of pieces by known designers, it may be best to live with slight damage in the interest of keeping the piece in original, and hence more valuable, condition.

Lacquered furniture can be refinished. However, the nature of the lacquer must be determined before it can be correctly stripped and/or fresh coats applied. A natural lacquer finish will be destroyed by any attempt to mix it with a synthetic. Cellulosic lacquers are difficult to apply by brush because each succeeding coat acts as a solvent on underlying coats. This causes the brush to drag over the surface. A new finish is best applied by a professional restorer experienced in lacquer work.

A Selective Glossary of Plastics Terms

The following terms and definitions were drawn from several sources, including *Modern Plastics Encyclopedia*, *A Manual of Plastics and Resins* edited by William Shack, and *Plastics* by J. Harry DuBois and Frederick W. John. In many cases definitions have been greatly simplified. Those who wish to pursue more complex definitions should refer further to the titles above and others relating to plastics technology in the bibliography. A bold-faced term within a definition indicates another glossary entry.

acetate. Common name for **cellulose acetate**.

acetone. A solvent used widely for many organic compounds and resins, including **cellulose nitrate** and most **acrylics**.

acrylic (acrylic resin). Common name for a group of **thermoplastic** resins known as acrylates or methacrylates. Most familiar methacrylates are crystal-clear products in the form of sheet, rod, tube, or moldings; but acrylics can also be colored, transparent or opaque. Most common acrylic trade names are **Plexiglas** and **Lucite**.

alpha cellulose. A pure form of **cellulose** prepared by chemical treatment. Used as a filler in urea and melamine resins.

amber. See **natural plastics**.

amino plastics. A general name for **urea-formaldehyde** and **melamine-formaldehyde** resins.

ashing. A finishing process generally used on **cast phenolics** in which wet grit, usually pumice, is applied to an object that is then buffed on a wheel.

Bakelite. Trade name for the first **thermosetting** phenol-formaldehyde resin, named for its synthesizer Dr. Leo Hendrick Baekeland (1863-1944) in 1909. Although still used generically to indicate "plastic," it is properly applied only to phenolic and other plastic materials produced by the Bakelite Corporation, later Union Carbide.

Beetle. Trade name for **urea-formaldehyde**. Also known as Beatl, Scarab, Bandalasta in England; Plaskon in the U.S.

Bernit. An imitation amber produced in Germany that contains extremely realistic features such as fissures, spangling, and plant and insect fragments; exact composition is unknown.

blanks; blanking. Another term for die-cutting in which sheet stock is cut to shape by means of dies on standard presses.

blow molding. A method of forming **thermoplastic** materials by forcing hot air into a hollow plastic tube, called a parison, until it expands and conforms to the shape of the mold cavity.

buffing. A final polishing in which polishing compounds and mild abrasives are applied to plastic surfaces with a rotating buffing wheel. See **ashing**.

calendering. The process of manufacturing, or forming, plastic sheet and film by compressing it to uniform thickness between counter-rotating rollers.

camphor. A substance obtained from the wood of the camphor tree that is used as a **plasticizer** for **cellulose nitrate**.

carbolic acid. Common name for **phenol**.

casein plastics. A hard hornlike plastic made from protein derived from skim milk that has been hardened by reacting it with formaldehyde. Once used extensively in the manufacture of buttons, buckles, and some jewelry under the now obsolete trade names of Aladdinite, Ameroid, Galorn, Galalith, and others.

cast; casting. The process of forming plastics without pressure by pouring the fluid resin into molds that are baked and cured. The hardened casting, in a variety of shapes such as tubes and rods, is then removed and machined, or **fabricated**, to create objects such as jewelry, handles, cases for radios, and other small objects.

cast phenolic resin. A thermosetting resin formed by pouring a fluid solution of **phenol-formaldehyde** into open molds where it hardens as it bakes at temperatures of 60–100°C. Commonly used in the 1930s and '40s in the manufacture of jewelry, it came in hundreds of colors, both translucent and opaque. Cast resins do not contain fillers, such as cotton fibers or wood flour, unlike the phenolic resins used for high-compression moldings, which are usually dark or mottled in color.

Catalin. A common trade name for **cast phenolic resin**, now obsolete.

cellophane. A plastic film composed of regenerated **cellulose** (a high grade chemical wood pulp), water, and a **plasticizer**, usually glycerol.

Celluloid. A trade name for **cellulose nitrate**, invented by John Wesley Hyatt in 1868.

cellulose. Fibrous material found in the cell walls of most plants, including dried woods, jute, hemp, flax, and cotton.

cellulose acetate. A tough **thermoplastic** material obtained by combining cellulose with acetic acid and acetic anhydride. Used widely in the manufacture of eyeglass frames, toothbrush backs, door knobs, toys; and in sheet form for lampshades and packaging.

cellulose acetate butyrate. An extremely tough, light, thermoplastic with good moisture resistance used for football helmets, tool handles, gun stocks, and other purposes. It is obtained by combining **cellulose** with acetic and butyric acids.

cellulose nitrate. The first man-made plastic material, commonly called **Celluloid**, created by the action of nitric and sulphuric acids on **cellulose**. The result is a brittle flake that is plasticized by **camphor** to create a doughy

substance that is generally formed into a block. Sheets are then planed and fabricated into such things as boxes, picture frames, and cutlery handles. Because of its high flammability, cellulose nitrate is now obsolete as a molding or forming material, having been supplanted by **cellulose acetate**.

compression molding. A technique for forming (mostly) thermoplastics by means of a two-part mold. The molding compound is placed into the lower half of a pre-heated steel cavity; the upper half is lowered and fixed in place. Heat and pressure applied over several minutes cause the compound to flow and conform to the shape of the inner surface of the mold, after which the plunger is raised and the molding ejected. See also **mold**.

die-cutting. See **blanking**.

Durez. A trade name for phenolic molding material.

ebonite. Natural rubber vulcanized to its maximum degree; moldable when mixed with softening agents.

edge lighting. A phenomenon in which diffuse light entering one edge of a transparent sheet of any pure transparent material denser than air, whose surfaces are clean, polished, and parallel, is reflected to the opposite edges. In plastics, the effect is best observed in acrylics and polystyrene.

epoxy. A complex family of thermosetting resins used widely for adhesives, architectural coatings, and flooring materials.

extrusion molding. A molding process used to produce tubes, rods, filaments, and film in a more or less continuous fashion. The molding compound is fed into a cylinder where a rotating screw forces it through an orifice much as toothpaste is extruded from its tube.

fabricating; fabrication. In plastics manufacture, a term used to describe the production of finished articles by means of machining rather than molding or casting. The techniques of plastics fabricating are similar to those used in working wood and metal, e.g., sawing, turning, drilling, carving, etc.

Fiberglas. A trade name for the glass fibers produced by the Owens-Corning Fiberglas Corporation used primarily in the production of fiberglass-reinforced plastic (FRP).

flow mark; flow line. An imperfection on the surface of a molded product, usually a wavy surface, caused by improper flow of the resin into the mold.

formaldehyde. A basic ingredient of some thermosetting resins. A clear, colorless gas, usually employed as a solution in water, it is derived from the oxidation of methanol or low boiling petroleum gases such as ethane, methane, propane, and butane.

gel coat. A resinous coating used to line open molds before the application of, for example, fiberglass reinforcing materials and polyester resin. The gel coat contains coloring agents and sets up with a high gloss.

glitter; flitter. Decorative sparkling flakes incorporated into the plastic during compounding, or molding.

gutta-percha. A rubberlike material, usually dark brown in color, obtained from the leaves and bark of tropical trees and once used widely as electrical insulation and for decorative moldings.

injection-molding. A molding process in which a heat-softened plastic material is rammed into a relatively cool closed cavity where it cures and is then quickly ejected. Used in mass-production of small objects such as jewelry, buttons, combs, toys, etc.

lacquer. A solution of natural or synthetic resins in rapidly evaporating solvents. On application, the solvent evaporates and leaves a hard protective coating with a high gloss. Synthetic lacquers are based on cellulose nitrate to which other resins and **plasticizers** are added. See **natural lacquer**.

laminate. A plastic material consisting of layers of resin-impregnated paper (or cloth, fiberglass, asbestos, or linen) that have been bonded together under heat and pressure to form a single sheet. Laminates are used industrially as electrical insulation and decoratively as facing for walls, cabinets, and table tops. In the latter case, the laminate is applied to wood or other surfaces by means of special adhesives. Thermosetting resins, such as **phenol-formaldehyde** and **melamine-formaldehyde**, which form acid-, heat-, and moisture-resistant surfaces are most commonly used in forming the laminate. The most familiar laminate brand name is Formica, which is often used generically.

linters. Short fibers that adhere to the cotton seed after ginning. Used in **rayon** manufacture, as fillers for plastics, as a base for the manufacture of cellulosic plastics.

Lucite. Trade name for **acrylic** manufactured by Du Pont.

Lumarith. A trade name for **cellulose acetate**.

Lustrex. A trade name for **polystyrene**.

Marblette. An obsolete trade name for **cast phenolic resin**.

melamine-formaldehyde. A thermosetting plastic derived from the reaction of melamine (derived from cyanamide or cyanuric chloride) and **formaldehyde**. An amino plastic with good moisture-resistance, it is used widely for the molding of tableware and for the decorative top layers of laminates.

mold; molding. (1) An open cavity in which molding material is placed and whose inner surface forms the outside shape of the finished, molded article. Molding occurs when a plunger forces the molding material against the inside surface of the mold. The outer shape of the plunger forms the inside shape of the molded object. (2) To shape products in a mold, usually under heat and pressure and for a specific amount of time during which the molding material, usually thermoset, is allowed to **polymerize**. See also **compression molding; injection molding**.

monomer. A relatively simple compound that can react to form a **polymer**.

mottle. Speckled or variegated coloring in plastics achieved by processing differently colored stocks together or by the addition of fillers such as wood flours or cloth fibers.

natural lacquer. Properly, resins obtained from the sap of trees native to China and Japan. These Oriental lacquers require slow and painstaking application of many layers, sometimes 20 or 30, each of which must dry in humid conditions to produce a characteristic gloss. Natural lacquers are distinct from **shellacs** and varnishes, which are more properly termed finishes. These are obtained from a secretion of the Burmese lac beetle, **coccus lacca**, and from copal, an amberlike tree resin.

natural plastics. Resins and other substances derived from plant or animal sources that have molding properties. They include (1) amber—a fossilized tree resin, (2) shellac—an insect secretion; (3) animal protein substances such as ivory, horn, and tortoiseshell.

nylon. A thermoplastic resin obtained from organic compounds called polyamides that can be formed into yarns and fibers, but which also can be injection-molded.

pearlessence. A mother-of-pearl simulation composed of guanine—a crystalline substance extracted from fish scales—combined with cellulosic, **acrylic** or **polystyrene** resins.

phenol. Carbolic acid, which is a basic compound used in synthesizing **phenol-formaldehyde** resins.

phenol-formaldehyde; phenolic resin. A synthetic thermosetting resin known familiarly by the trade names Bakelite, Durez, Durite, Indur, Resinox, and others. Used for moldings and also as an impregnating agent and as a component of paints, varnishes, lacquers, and adhesives.

plastic. Broadly, any material that can be shaped under heat and pressure; in the strict modern sense, a synthetic organic compound known as a **polymer**.

plasticizer. A chemical agent incorporated into a plastic substance before molding to make it softer and more flexible.

Plexiglas. Trade name for acrylic resin produced by the Rohm & Haas Company.

polybern. An amber imitation that combines real amber chips with polyester resin; developed in Germany and produced in Poland and Lithuania.

polycarbonate. A high-performance, extremely strong thermoplastic that is a polyester of carbonic acid. It is resistant to water and stains from acids contained in foods; it is also flame resistant and can be made as transparent as glass or opaque. Some consumer uses include food and liquid containers, tableware, toys, and solar collectors.

polyester. A thermosetting resin formed by the reaction between an acid and an alcohol, both organic. Extremely strong and hard, with dimensional stability and minimal water absorption, polyester resins cure without pressure or heat and thus can be cast in low-cost open molds or used to produce laminates and reinforced plastics of exceptional size and contour, such as ships' hulls. See also **Fiberglas**.

polyethylene. A tough, waxy thermoplastic material derived from polymers of ethylene, a hydrocarbon derived from coal gas or obtained from the action of concentrated sulphuric acid on alcohol. In film form it is used for transparent food wrapping and for packaging pharmaceuticals because of its unusual chemical-, puncture-, and moisture-resistance. These same qualities make it an excellent electrical insulation material and molding material for toys and furniture.

polymer. A giant or macro-molecule formed when single molecules—**monomers**—link up or bond to each other.

polystyrene. A thermoplastic polymer obtained from ethylene. It has excellent electrical insulating properties, fine clarity, and wide color-range. Used extensively for housewares, toys, and packaging.

polyvinyl chloride (PVC). A thermoplastic resin derived from a gas obtained from the reaction of acetylene and hydrogen chloride. PVC is familiar in film form as shower curtain material; in extruded tube form as electrical insulation pipe.

Pyralin. A trade name for **cellulose nitrate**.

Pyroxylin. Cellulose nitrate.

rayon. A term that describes fibers made from regenerated cellulose, called viscose rayon; and from cellulose acetate, called rayon acetate (trade names Celanese and others); and from cellulose triacetate. Viscose rayon fiber was first spun in 1911; rayon acetate was first spun in France in 1918, although not produced in America until 1925.

reinforced plastics. Resins strengthened, or reinforced, with materials such as glass fibers, and fillers such as minerals and wood flour.

resin. A solid or semisolid organic product, either natural or synthetic, with no definite melting point and amorphous structure. Most resins are insoluble in water.

rubber. Natural rubber, or latex, is a milky substance with elastic properties obtained from tropical plants. It is described chemically as a hydrocarbon. Although rubber has many plastic qualities such as moldability, it is categorized for its elasticity as an elastomer. See also **silicone**.

shellac. A natural resin excreted by an insect indigenous to Burma and India (see **natural lacquers**). It is a thermoplastic when fresh but becomes thermosetting at room temperature. Shellac becomes a molding compound when mixed with a filler such as wood flour.

silicone. A versatile family of polymeric materials that are partly organic and partly inorganic. They resist solvents and offer lubricity. They combine with many types of organic substances, making possible a range of diverse products from silicone rubbers used in electrical insulation to soft contact lenses. FDA-approved silicone lenses transmit more oxygen to the eye than any other type of contact lens.

Slocum. A synthetic resin produced by J. L. Slocum Laboratories in Michigan for use by jewelers as imitation amber. Patty D. Rice describes it as having insect inclusions and "sun-spangle" fissures that characterize true amber.

spray-up; hand lay-up. A molding technique in which an operator uses a spray gun to line a mold with resin and/or reinforcing material such as glass fibers, sometimes simultaneously. Large-size moldings such as boat hulls and modular architectural units are often produced by spray-up, although it is most commonly used today to produce prototypes. See also **gel coat**; **reinforced plastics**.

thermoforming. A process in which a thermoplastic sheet is first heated, then forced down on a mold surface—either by vacuum action or compression, or both—where it cools and retains the mold shape.

thermoplastic. A plastic substance that can be repeatedly softened by heat after it has been hardened by cooling. Examples include the cellulosic plastics, **acrylics**, styrenes, **polyethylenes**, **vinyls**, and **nylons**.

thermoset. A synthetic resin that becomes hard and infusible when subjected to heat and pressure and thus cannot be softened and reshaped. Examples include the phenolics and amino resins and many other compounds, including **polyesters**, **silicones**, **epoxies**, **caseins**, and some types of **urethanes**.

transfer molding. A molding technique in which the molding compound is first heated in a chamber, then forced under high pressure, or transferred, into the closed mold where it cures.

urea-formaldehyde. A thermosetting resin derived from the reaction of urea (an ammonia compound) and formaldehyde. Its molding properties are similar to phenolic resins, with the exception that ureas can be produced in a wider variety of colors that include pure white and pastels.

urethane. See **polyurethane**.

vinyl. Common name for a group of synthetic thermoplastic resins that include **polyvinyl chloride (PVC)**. Vinyl in sheet form is often referred to as vinylite.

Bibliography

Ambasz, Emilio, ed. *Italy: The New Domestic Landscape*. (Catalog of exhibition at Museum of Modern Art, May 26-Sept. 11, 1972.) New York: The Museum of Modern Art, in collaboration with Centro Di, Florence, 1972.

Anderton, Johana Gast. *More Twentieth Century Dolls, from Bisque to Vinyl*. North Kansas City, Missouri: Athena Publishing Co., 1974.

————. *Twentieth Century Dolls, from Bisque to Vinyl*. North Kansas City, Missouri: Trojan Press, 1974.

Baer, Eric, ed. *Engineering Design for Plastics*. New York: Reinhold Publishing Corp., 1964.

Bailey, Chris H. *Two Hundred Years of American Clocks and Watches*. New Jersey: Prentice-Hall, 1975.

Bakeliet: Techniek, Vormgeving, Gebruik. (Bakelite: Technique, Form, and Material). Rotterdam: catalog of exhibition at Boymans-van Beuningen Museum, May 23–July 20, 1981.

Baldinger, Wallace S. *The Visual Arts*. New York: Holt, Rinehart & Winston, 1960.

Banham, Reyner. *Design By Choice*. Penny Sparke, ed. New York: Rizzoli, 1981.

Battersby, Martin. *The Decorative Twenties*. New York: Collier/Macmillan, 1961.

————. *The Decorative Thirties*. New York: Walker, 1971.

Bayley, Stephen, ed. *In Good Shape: Style in Industrial Products 1900 to 1960*. New York: Van Nostrand Reinhold, 1979.

Beck, Ronald D. *Plastic Product Design*, 2nd ed. New York: Van Nostrand Reinhold, 1980.

Beer, Eilene Harrison. *Scandinavian Design: Objects of a Lifestyle*. New York: Farrar, Straus & Giroux/The American-Scandinavian Foundation, 1975.

Bradford, Peter, and Barbara Prete, eds. *The Chair: The current state of the art with the who, the why, and the what of it*. New York: Thomas Y. Crowell, 1978.

Brown, Curtis, F. *Star-Spangled Kitsch*. New York: Universe Books, 1975.

Burkhardt, François, and Inez Franksen, eds. *Design: Dieter Rams*. Gerhardt Verlag, 1980, 1981.

Bush, Donald J. *The Streamlined Decade*. New York: Braziller, 1975.

Caplan, Ralph. *The Design of Herman Miller*. New York: Whitney Library of Design/Watson-Guptill, 1976.

Carpenter, Edward K. *Industrial Design, 25th Annual Design Review*. New York: Whitney Library of Design/Watson-Guptill, 1979.

Carrington, Noel, ed. *British Achievement in Design*, specifically the chapter "Plastics" by E. G. Couzens. The Pilot Press, 1946.

Carter, Ernestine. *The Changing World of Fashion: From 1900 to the Present*. New York: Putnam, 1977.

Century of Fashion, A, 1880–1980. Minneapolis: Minnesota Museum of Art, 1980.

Cheney, Sheldon, and Martha Candler Cheney. *Art and the Machine: An Account of Industrial Design in 20th-Century America*. New York: Whittlesey House, 1936.

Chester, Giraud, Garnet R. Garrison, Edgar E. Willis. *Television and Radio*, 3rd ed. New York: Appleton-Century-Crofts, 1963.

Cunnington, C. Willet. *Englishwomen's Clothing of the Present Century*. London: Faber & Faber, 1952.

Davies, Karen. *At Home in Manhattan: Modern Decorative Arts, 1925 to the Depression*. New Haven: Yale University Art Gallery, 1983.

Dean, Barry. *Design Review; Industrial Design, 27th Annual*. Whitney Library of Design/Watson-Guptill/Architectural Press, 1978.

Derieux, Mary, and Isabelle Stevenson. *The Complete Book of Interior Decorating*. New York: Greystone Press, 1949.

Design Collection, The; Selected Objects. New York: The Museum of Modern Art.

Design '46: "Britain Can Make It" Exhibition. London: Council of Industrial Design, 1946.

Designs of Raymond Loewy, The. Washington, D.C.: published for the Renwick Gallery of the National Collection of Fine Arts by the Smithsonian Press, 1975.

Doblin, Jay. *100 Great Product Designs.* New York: Van Nostrand Reinhold, 1970.

DuBois, J. Harry. *Plastics History U.S.A.* Boston: Chaners Books, 1972.

————, and Frederick W. John. *Plastics,* 6th ed. New York: Van Nostrand Reinhold, 1981.

Duffin, D. J. *Laminated Plastic,* 2nd ed. New York: Reinhold Publishing Corporation, 1966.

Duncan, Alastair. *Art Nouveau and Art Deco Lighting.* New York: Simon and Schuster, 1978.

Du Pont: The Autobiography of An American Enterprise. Wilmington: E. I. du Pont de Nemours & Company, 1952.

Encyclopedia of Collectibles, volumes 1–16. Alexandria: Time-Life Books, 1977–1980.

Everyday Arts Quarterly, No. 6, Winter 1947–48. Minneapolis: Walker Art Center.

Fabulous Fashion 1907–1967. New York: Costume Institute, Metropolitan Museum of Art, 1967.

Fielding, T. J. *History of Bakelite Limited.* London: Bakelite Limited, undated.

Foa, Linda, and Geri Brin. *Kids' Stuff.* New York: Pantheon, 1979.

Frankl, Paul T. *Form and Re-Form: A Practical Handbook of Modern Interiors.* New York: Harper, 1930.

————. *New Dimensions: The Decorative Arts Today* (1928). New York: Da Capo, 1975.

Friedmann, Arnold, John F. Pile, and Forrest Wilson. *Interior Design: An Introduction to Architectural Interiors.* New York: Elsevier, 1982.

Garner, Phillippe. *Contemporary Decorative Arts, from 1940 to the Present.* New York: Facts on File, Inc., 1980.

Giedion, Sigfried. *Mechanization Takes Command: A Contribution to Anonymous History.* New York: Oxford University Press, 1948.

Gloag, John. *Plastics and Industrial Design;* with a section on the different types of plastics, their properties and uses, by Grace Lovat Fraser. London: George Allen & Unwin, Ltd., 1945.

Grief, Martin. *Depression Modern: The Thirties Style in America.* New York: Universe Books, 1975.

Hanks, David A. *Innovative Furniture in America from 1800 to the Present.* New York: Horizon Press, 1981.

Hanks, David A., and Derek Ostergard. *Gilbert Rohde.* New York: Washburn Gallery, 1981.

Heide, Robert, and John Gilman. *Dime-Store Dream Parade: Popular Culture 1925–1955.* New York: Dutton, 1979.

Heisinger, Kathryn B. *Design Since 1945.* (An exhibition at Philadelphia Museum of Art, Oct. 16, 1983–Jan. 8, 1984) New York: Rizzoli, 1983.

Hemline, Neckline, Streamline: Women's Fashions 1890-1940. From the Collection of Beverly Birks. Museum of Art, Pennsylvania State University, 1981.

Hennessey, William J. *Russel Wright, American Designer.* Cambridge: The MIT Press, 1983.

Heskett, John. *Industrial Design.* New York and Toronto: Oxford University Press, 1980.

Hillier, Bevis. *The Decorative Arts of the Forties and Fifties: Austerity/Binge.* New York: Clarkson N. Potter, 1975.

————. *The World of Art Deco.* (An Exhibition organized by Minneapolis Institute of Arts, July–September, 1971.) New York: Dutton, 1971.

Hollander, Harry. *Plastics for Jewelry.* New York: Watson-Guptil, 1977.

Howell, Georgina. *In Vogue.* New York: Schocken Books, 1976.

Hughes, Robert. *The Shock of the New.* New York: Alfred A. Knopf, 1981.

Industrial Design in America, 1954. Society of Industrial Designers, ed. New York: Farrar, Straus & Young, 1954.

Inventive Clothes 1909–1939. New York: exhibition sponsored by Metropolitan Museum of Art, 1975.

Arne Jacobsen, A Danish Architect. Danish Ministry of Foreign Affairs, 1971/72.

Arne Jacobsen. Danish Bicentennial Committee, 1976.

Katz, Sylvia. *Classic Plastics.* London: Thames and Hudson, 1984.

————. *Plastics: Designs and Materials.* London: Studio Vista, 1978.

Kellaway, T. W., and N. P. Meadway. *Introducing Plastics.* A John A. Crowther Publication, 1944.

Kerr, Ann. *Russel Wright and His Dinnerware: A Descriptive Price Guide.* Sidney, Ohio, 1981.

Knoll au Louvre. Paris: catalog of exhibition at Pavillon de Marsan, Musée des Arts Decoratifs, 1972.

Kron, Joan, and Suzanne Slesin. *High Tech: The Industrial Style Source Book for the Home.* New York: Clarkson Potter, 1978.

Lamarova, Milena. *Design and Plastics.* Prague: an Exhibition at Museum of Decorative Arts, Oct.–Dec., 1972.

Larrabee, Eric, and Massimo Vignelli. *Knoll Design.* New York: Abrams, 1981.

Larson, Leslie. *Lighting and Its Design.* New York: Whitney Library of Design, 1964.

Lawrence, Cliff. *Fountain Pens: History, Repair and Current Values.* Paducah, Kentucky: Collector Books, 1977.

Leonard, R. I., and C. A. Glassgold, eds. *Annual of American Design, 1931.* New York: Ives Washburn, 1930.

Lesieutre, Alain. *The Spirit and Splendor of Art Deco.* London: Paddington Press, 1974.

Lifshey, Earl. *The Housewares Story: A History of the American Housewares Industry.* Chicago: National Housewares Manufacturers Association, 1973.

Lindbeck, John R. *Designing Today's Manufactured Products*. Bloomington, Illinois: McKnight & McKnight Publishing Co., 1972.

Lindkvist, Lennart, ed. *Design in Sweden*. The Swedish Institute in collaboration with the Swedish Society of Industrial Design, 1977.

Loewy, Raymond. *Never Leave Well Enough Alone*. New York: Simon & Schuster, 1951.

Lynes, Russell. *Good Old Modern: An Intimate Portrait of the Museum of Modern Art*. New York: Atheneum, 1973.

————. *The Tastemakers*. New York: Grosset & Dunlap, 1954.

McClintock, Inez and Michael. *Toys in America*. Washington, D.C.: Public Affairs Press, 1961.

McMahon, Morgan E. *A Flick of the Switch: 1930–1950*. Palos Verdes Peninsula, California: Vintage Radio, 1975.

————. *Vintage Radio: 1887–1929*. Vintage Radio, 1973.

Meadmore, Clement. *The Modern Chair: Classics in Production*. New York: Van Nostrand Reinhold, 1975.

Meikle, Jeffrey L. *Twentieth Century Limited: Industrial Design in America, 1925–1939*. Philadelphia: Temple University Press, 1979.

Menten, Theodore. *The Art Deco Style*. New York: Dover, 1972.

Modern Plastics Encyclopedia 1982–83. New York: McGraw-Hill, 1983.

Nelson, George. *Problems of Design*. New York: Whitney Publications, 1957.

Newman, Thelma R. *Plastics As An Art Form*. New York: Chilton, 1972.

————. *Plastics As Design Form*, rev. ed. New York: Chilton, 1969.

————, Jay Harley Newman, and Lee Scott Newman. *The Lamp and Lighting Book*. New York: Crown, 1976.

O'Higgins, Patrick. *Madame: An Intimate Biography of Helena Rubinstein*. New York: The Viking Press, 1971.

Page, Marian. *Furniture Designed by Architects*. New York: Whitney Library of Design, 1980.

Papanek, Victor. *Design for the Real World*. New York: Pantheon, 1971.

Phillips, Derek. *Lighting in Architectural Designs*. New York: McGraw-Hill, 1964.

Plastic as Plastic. New York: catalog of exhibition held at Museum of Contemporary Crafts, Nov. 23, 1968–Jan. 12, 1969.

Plastics Antiques. Three-part catalog of a traveling exhibition of Plastic Consumer Products from the 1850s to the 1950s. Sponsored by British Industrial Plastics Ltd., 1977.

Pool, Mary Jane, ed. *20th Century Decorating, Architecture & Gardens: 80 Years of Ideas & Pleasure from House & Garden*. New York: Holt, Rinehart & Winston, 1980.

Pulos, Arthur J. *American Design Ethic: A History of Industrial Design to 1940*. Cambridge: The MIT Press, 1983.

Quarmby, Arthur. *Plastics and Architecture*. New York: Praeger, 1974.

Rabolini, Anna. *Gli Anni Plastici* (The Plastic Years). Milan: catalog of exhibition held at the Rodolfo II Gallery, Nov.–Dec., 1982. Gruppo Montedison, 1983.

Read, Herbert. *Art & Industry*. Bloomington: Indiana University Press, 1961.

Rice, Patty D. *Amber: The Golden Gem of the Ages*. New York: Van Nostrand Reinhold, 1980.

Rosen, Stephen L. *Fundamental Principles of Polymeric Materials*. New York: John Wiley & Sons, 1982.

Sasso, John, and Michael H. Brown, Jr. *Plastics in Practice: A Handbook of Product Applications*. New York: McGraw-Hill, 1945.

Schack, William, ed. *A Manual of Plastics and Resins*. Brooklyn: Chemical Publishing Co., 1950.

Schiaparelli, Elsa. *Shocking Life*. New York: Dutton, 1954.

Sembach, Klaus-Jurgen. *Contemporary Furniture*. New York: Architectural Book Publishing Company, 1982.

————. *Style 1930: Elegance and Sophistication in Architecture, Design, Fashion, Graphics and Photography*. New York: Universe Books, 1971.

Simonds, Herbert R., and M. H. Bigelow. *The New Plastics*. New York: D. Van Nostrand Company, 1945.

Slesin, Suzanne. *French Style*. New York: Clarkson N. Potter, 1982.

Sparke, Penny. *Ettore Sottsass, Jnr*. London: The Design Council, 1982.

Steele, Gerald L. *Exploring the World of Plastics*. Bloomington, Illinois: McKnight Publishing Co., 1977.

Teague, Walter Dorwin. *Design This Day*. New York: Harcourt Brace, 1940.

This Fabulous Century, vol. IV, 1930–1940. New York: Time-Life Books.

U.S. Industrial Design 1951. Society of Industrial Designers, ed. New York: Studio Publications and Thomas Y. Crowell, 1951.

Van Doren, Harold. *Industrial Design, A Practical Guide*. New York: McGraw-Hill, 1940.

Wallance, Don. *Shaping America's Products*. New York: Reinhold Publishing, 1956.

Watson, Sir Francis, intro. *The History of Furniture*. New York: Crescent Books, 1976.

Whiteman, Von. *Looking Back At Fashion, 1901–1939*. London: EP Publishing Limited, 1978.

Wilcox, R. Turner. *The Dictionary of Costume*. New York: Charles Scribner's Sons, 1969.

Wilk, Christopher. *Thonet: 150 Years of Furniture*. Westbury, New York: Barron's, 1980.

Willcox, Donald J. *Finnish Design: Facts and Fancy*. New York: Van Nostrand Reinhold, 1973.

Wilson, Eunice. *A History of Shoe Fashions*. New York: Pitman/Theater Arts, 1969.

Wolfe, Tom. *From Bauhaus to Our House*. New York: Farrar, Straus & Giroux, 1981.

Index

(Numbers in italic type refer to illustrations)